# CAPTAIN AMERICA

## THE TRIAL OF CAPTAIN AMERICA

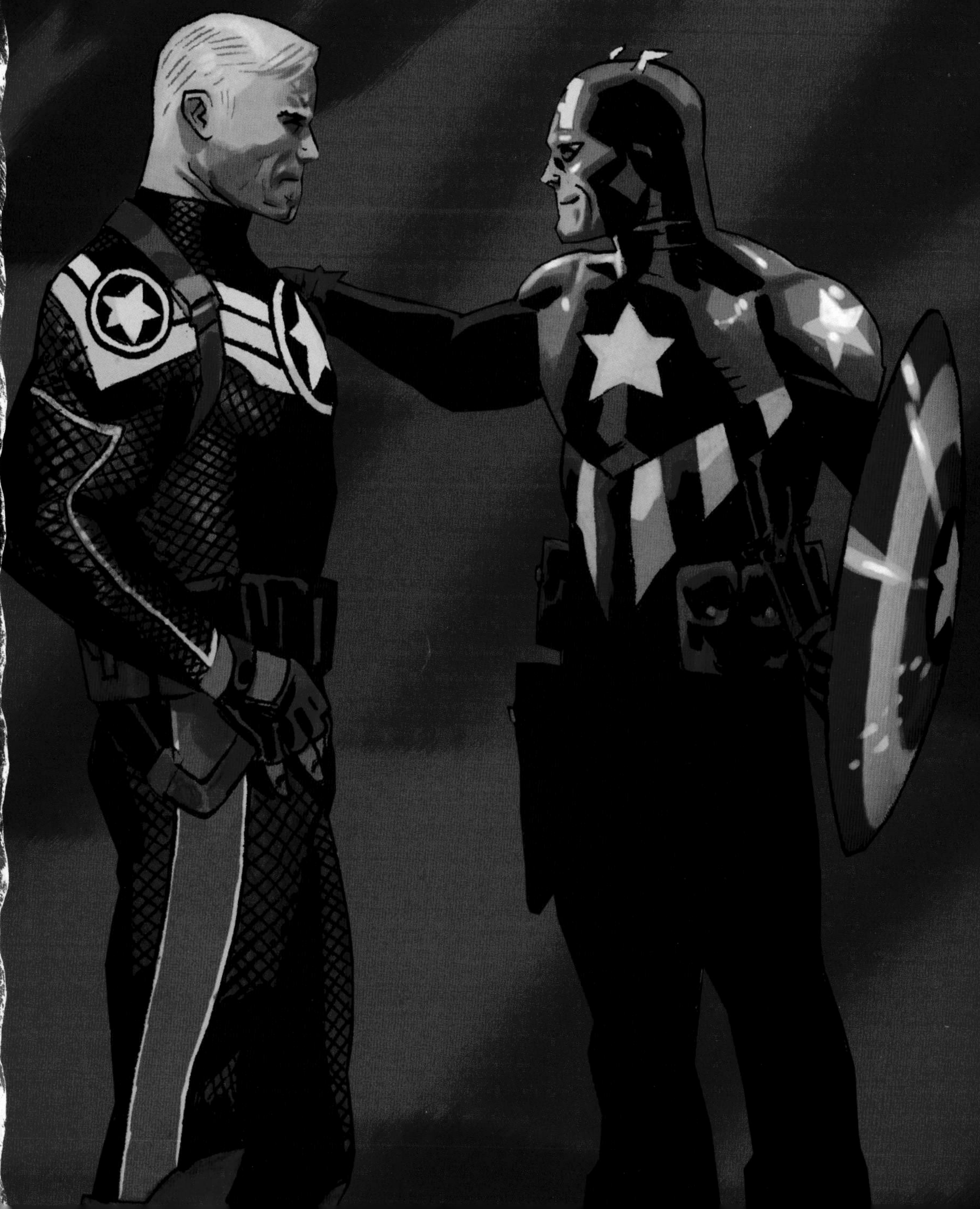

# CAPTAIN AMERICA

## THE TRIAL OF CAPTAIN AMERICA

**WRITER: Ed Brubaker**

**ART & COLORS**, ISSUE #611: **Daniel Acuña**

**PENCILS**, ISSUES #612-615: **Butch Guice**

**INKS**, ISSUES #612-615:

**Butch Guice & Stefano Gaudiano**
with **Rick Magyar, Mark Morales,
Tom Palmer & Mike Perkins**

**COLORS**, ISSUES #612-615: **Bettie Breitweiser**
with **Frank Martin, Chris Sotomayor & Jay David Ramos**

**ART & COLORS**, ISSUE #615.1: **Mitch Breitweiser**

**COLORS**, ISSUES #612-615: **Bettie Breitweiser**

**LETTERER: VC's Joe Caramagna**

**COVER ART: Marko Djurdjevic & Daniel Acuña** (Issue #615.1)

**ASSOCIATE EDITOR: Lauren Sankovitch**

**EDITOR: Tom Brevoort**

**Captain America created by Joe Simon & Jack Kirby**

---

Collection Editor: Jennifer Grünwald
Editorial Assistants: James Emmett & Joe Hochstein
Assistant Editors: Alex Starbuck & Nelson Ribeiro
Editor, Special Projects: Mark D. Beazley
Senior Editor, Special Projects: Jeff Youngquist
Senior Vice President of Sales: David Gabriel

Editor in Chief: Axel Alonso • Chief Creative Officer: Joe Quesada
Publisher: Dan Buckley • Executive Producer: Alan Fine

**CAPTAIN AMERICA: THE TRIAL OF CAPTAIN AMERICA.** Contains material originally published in magazine form as CAPTAIN AMERICA #611-615 and #615.1. First printing 2011. Hardcover ISBN# 978-0-7851-5119-7. Softcover ISBN# 978-0-7851-5120-3. Published by MARVEL WORLDWIDE, INC., a subsidiary of MARVEL ENTERTAINMENT, LLC. OFFICE OF PUBLICATION: 135 West 50th Street, New York, NY 10020. Copyright © 2010 and 2011 Marvel Characters, Inc. All rights reserved. Hardcover: $24.99 per copy in the U.S. and $27.99 in Canada (GST #R127032852). Softcover: $19.99 per copy in the U.S. and $21.99 in Canada (GST #R127032852). Canadian Agreement #40668537. All characters featured in this issue and the distinctive names and likenesses thereof, and all related indicia are trademarks of Marvel Characters, Inc. No similarity between any of the names, characters, persons, and/or institutions in this magazine with those of any living or dead person or institution is intended, and any such similarity which may exist is purely coincidental. **Printed in the U.S.A.** ALAN FINE, EVP - Office of the President, Marvel Worldwide, Inc. and EVP & CMO Marvel Characters B.V.; DAN BUCKLEY, Publisher & President - Print, Animation & Digital Divisions; JOE QUESADA, Chief Creative Officer; JIM SOKOLOWSKI, Chief Operating Officer; DAVID BOGART, SVP of Business Affairs & Talent Management; TOM BREVOORT, SVP of Publishing; C.B. CEBULSKI, SVP of Creator & Content Development; DAVID GABRIEL, SVP of Publishing Sales & Circulation; MICHAEL PASCIULLO, SVP of Brand Planning & Communications; JIM O'KEEFE, VP of Operations & Logistics; DAN CARR, Executive Director of Publishing Technology; JUSTIN F. GABRIE, Director of Publishing & Editorial Operations; SUSAN CRESPI, Editorial Operations Manager; ALEX MORALES, Publishing Operations Manager; STAN LEE, Chairman Emeritus. For information regarding advertising in Marvel Comics or on Marvel.com, please contact Ron Stern, VP of Business Development, at rstern@marvel.com. For Marvel subscription inquiries, please call 800-217-9158. **Manufactured between 3/14/2011 and 4/11/2011 (hardcover), and 3/14/2011 and 10/10/2011 (softcover), by R.R. DONNELLEY, INC., SALEM, VA, USA.**

10 9 8 7 6 5 4 3 2 1

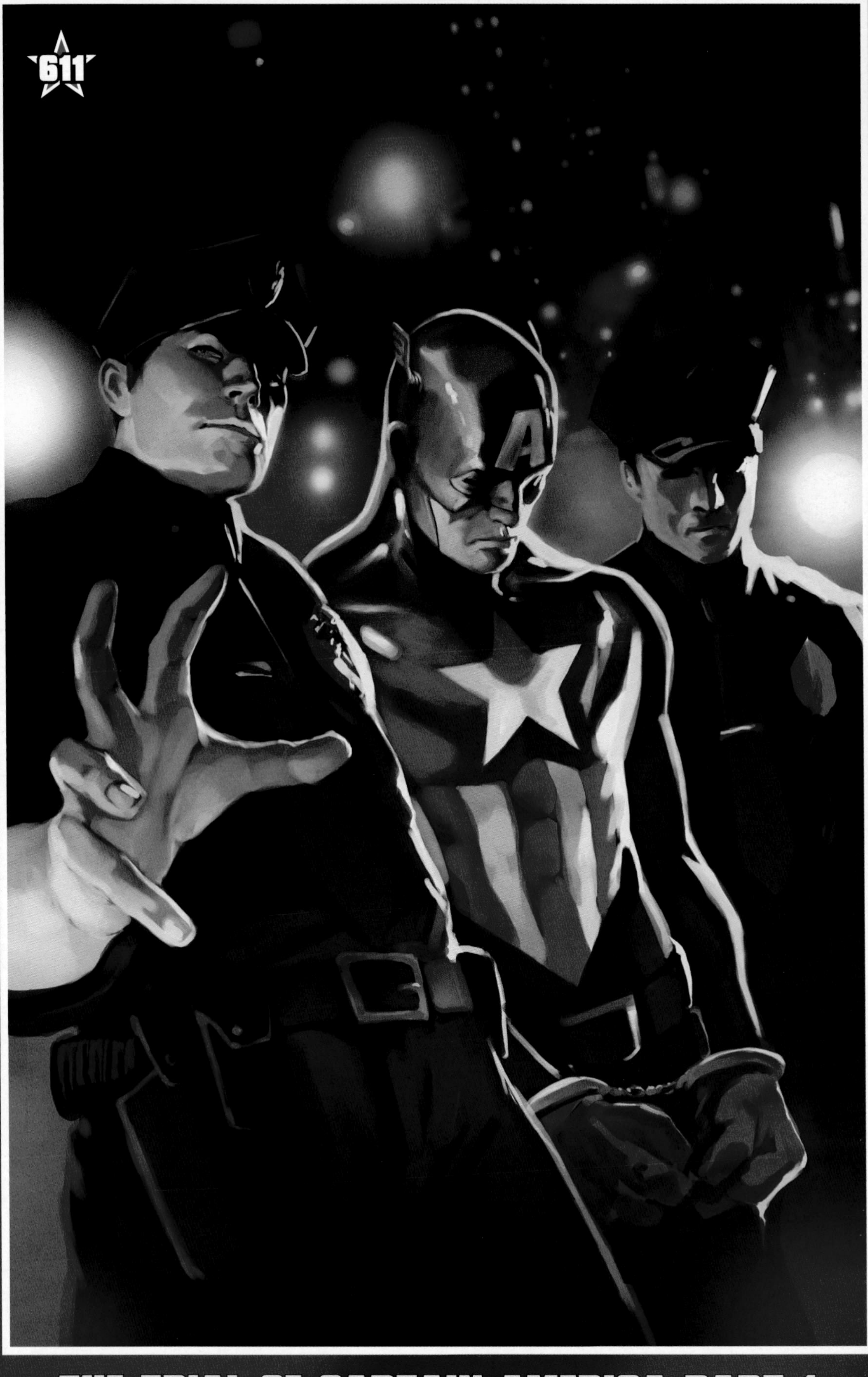
611

THE TRIAL OF CAPTAIN AMERICA PART 1

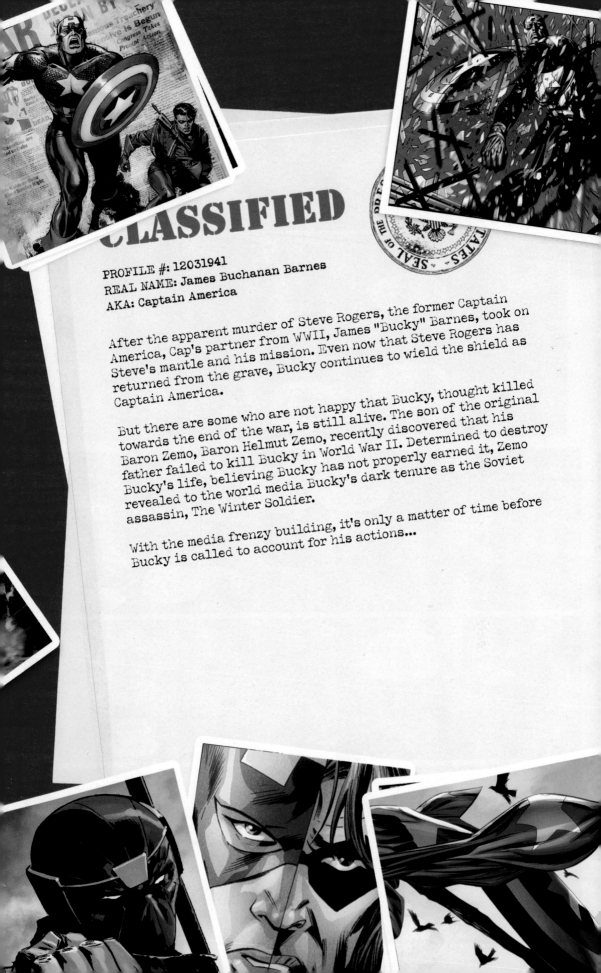

# CLASSIFIED

PROFILE #: 12031941
REAL NAME: James Buchanan Barnes
AKA: Captain America

After the apparent murder of Steve Rogers, the former Captain America, Cap's partner from WWII, James "Bucky" Barnes, took on Steve's mantle and his mission. Even now that Steve Rogers has returned from the grave, Bucky continues to wield the shield as Captain America.

But there are some who are not happy that Bucky, thought killed towards the end of the war, is still alive. The son of the original Baron Zemo, Baron Helmut Zemo, recently discovered that his father failed to kill Bucky in World War II. Determined to destroy Bucky's life, believing Bucky has not properly earned it, Zemo revealed to the world media Bucky's dark tenure as the Soviet assassin, The Winter Soldier.

With the media frenzy building, it's only a matter of time before Bucky is called to account for his actions...

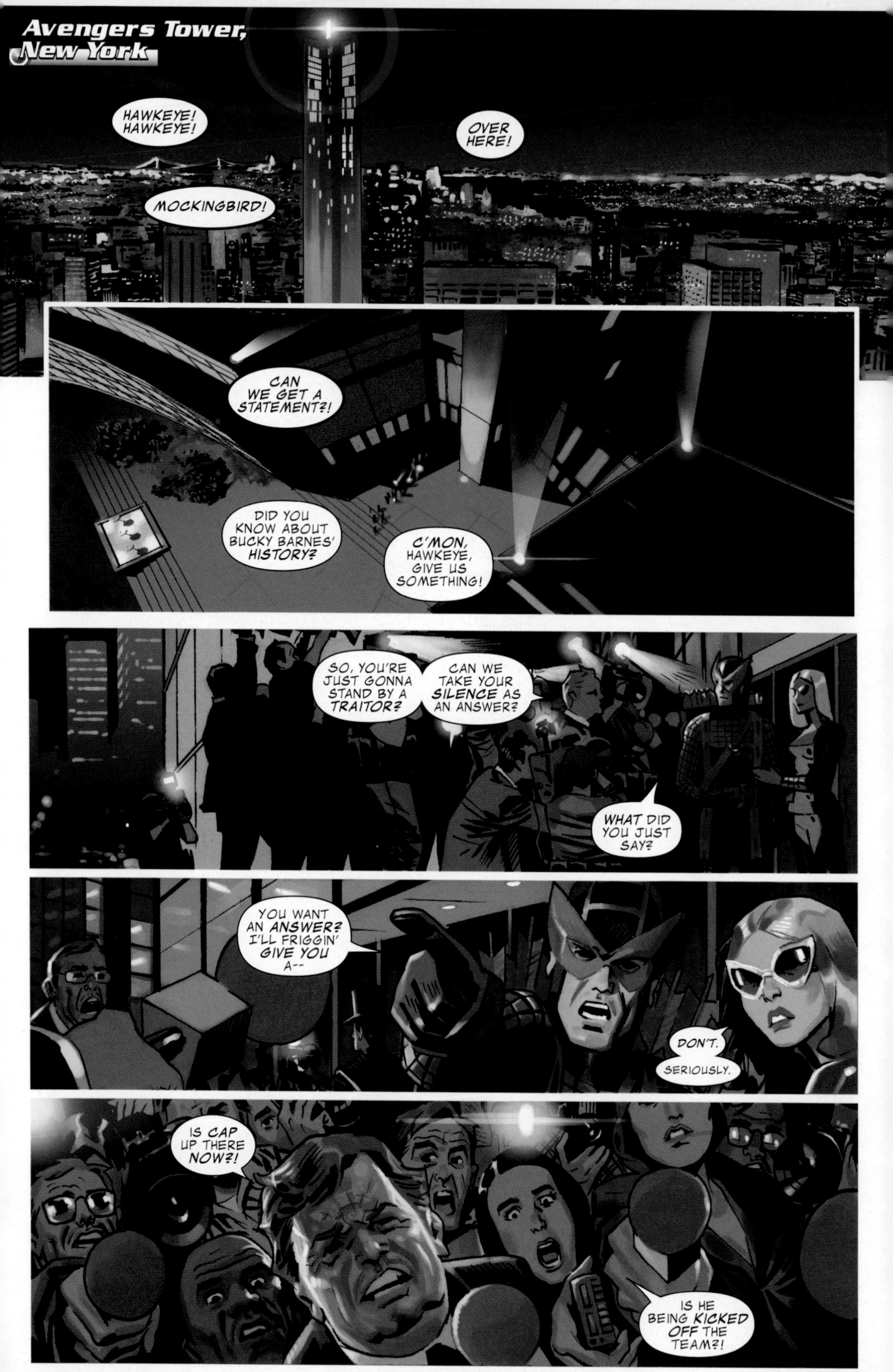
Avengers Tower, New York
HAWKEYE! HAWKEYE!
OVER HERE!
MOCKINGBIRD!
CAN WE GET A STATEMENT?!
DID YOU KNOW ABOUT BUCKY BARNES' HISTORY?
C'MON, HAWKEYE, GIVE US SOMETHING!
SO, YOU'RE JUST GONNA STAND BY A TRAITOR?
CAN WE TAKE YOUR SILENCE AS AN ANSWER?
WHAT DID YOU JUST SAY?
YOU WANT AN ANSWER? I'LL FRIGGIN' GIVE YOU A--
DON'T.
SERIOUSLY.
IS CAP UP THERE NOW?!
IS HE BEING KICKED OFF THE TEAM?!

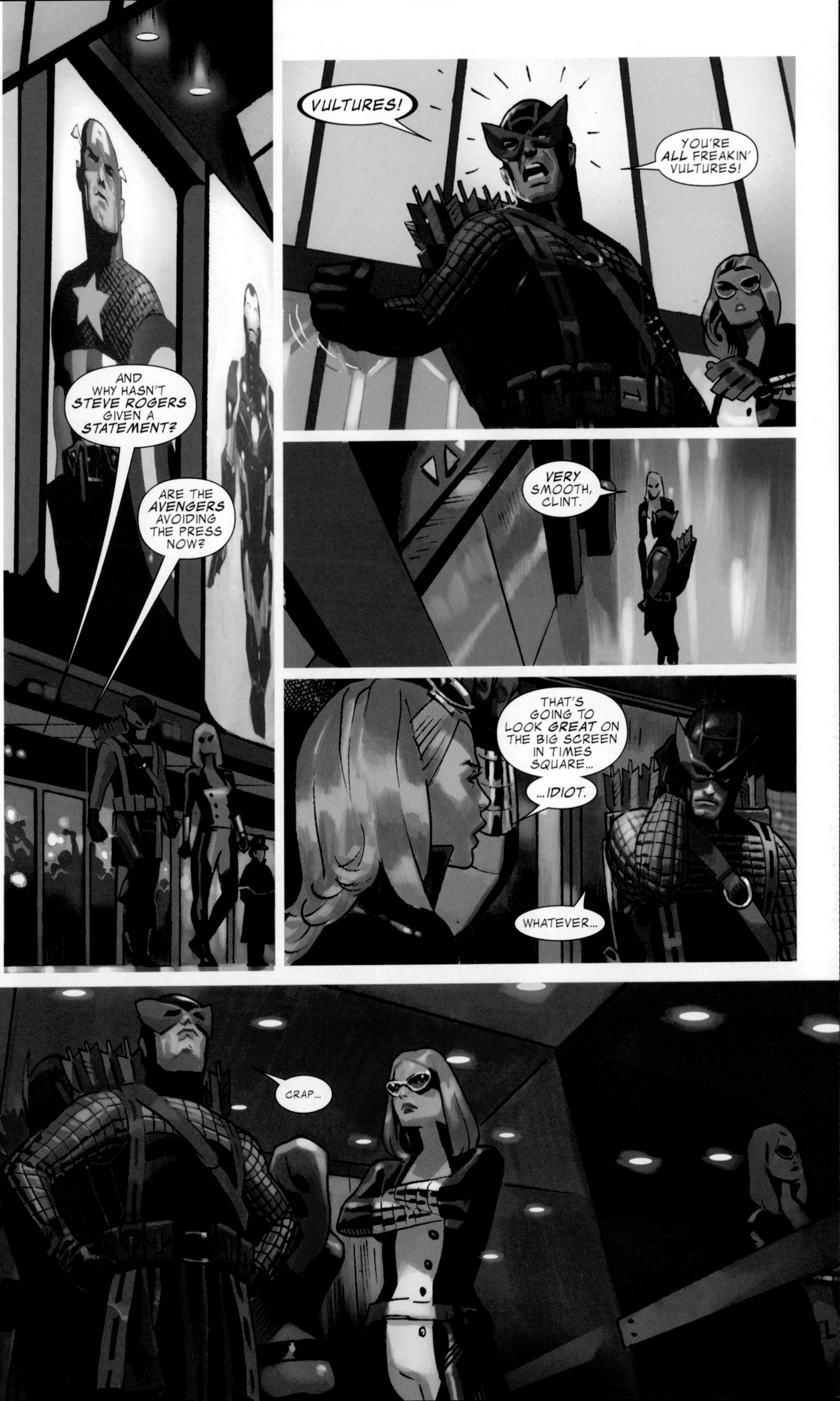

AND WHY HASN'T STEVE ROGERS GIVEN A STATEMENT?
ARE THE AVENGERS AVOIDING THE PRESS NOW?
VULTURES!
YOU'RE ALL FREAKIN' VULTURES!
VERY SMOOTH, CLINT.
THAT'S GOING TO LOOK GREAT ON THE BIG SCREEN IN TIMES SQUARE...
...IDIOT.
WHATEVER...
CRAP...

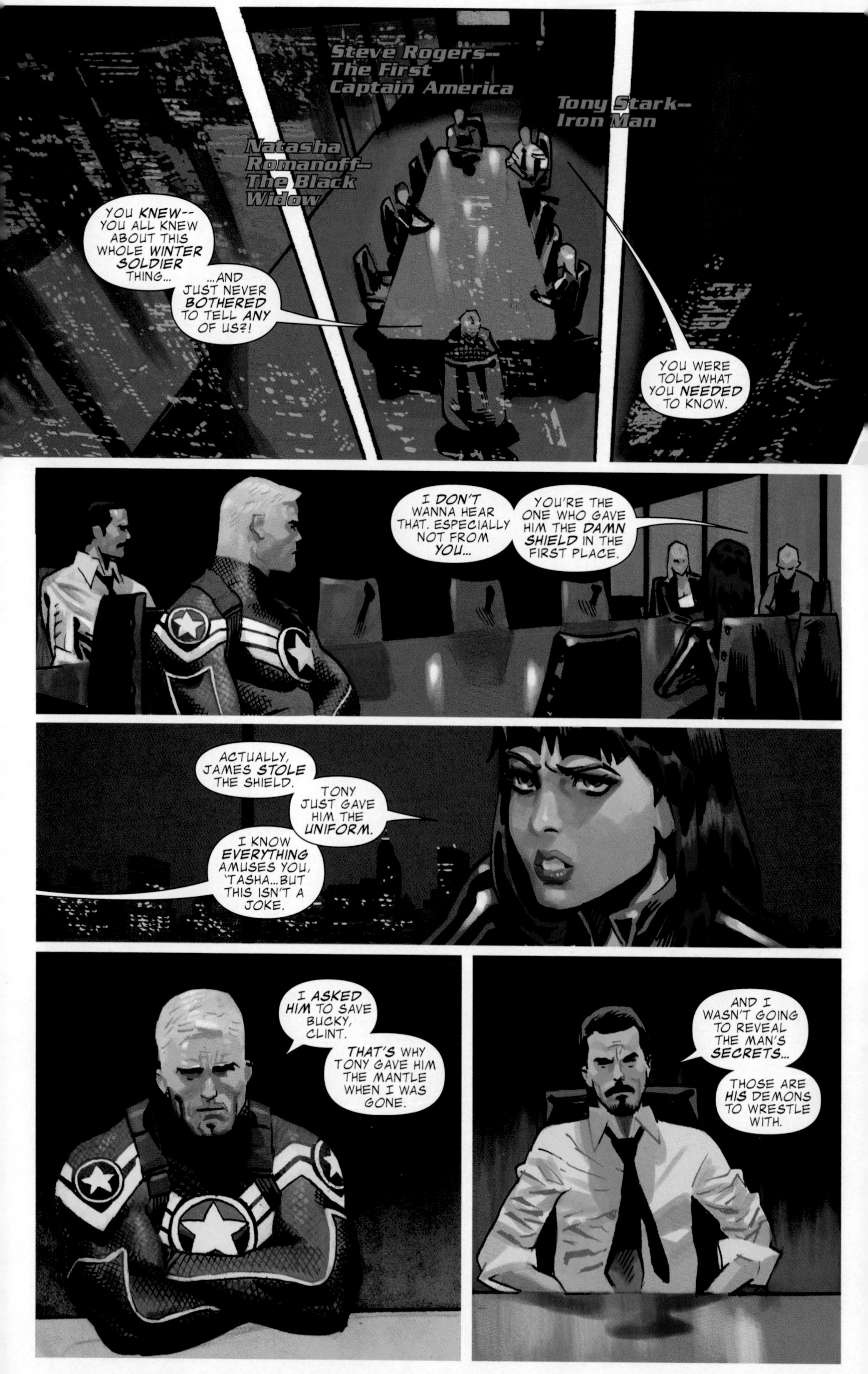
Steve Rogers-- The First Captain America
Tony Stark-- Iron Man
Natasha Romanoff-- The Black Widow
YOU KNEW-- YOU ALL KNEW ABOUT THIS WHOLE WINTER SOLDIER THING...
...AND JUST NEVER BOTHERED TO TELL ANY OF US?!
YOU WERE TOLD WHAT YOU NEEDED TO KNOW.
I DON'T WANNA HEAR THAT. ESPECIALLY NOT FROM YOU...
YOU'RE THE ONE WHO GAVE HIM THE DAMN SHIELD IN THE FIRST PLACE.
ACTUALLY, JAMES STOLE THE SHIELD.
TONY JUST GAVE HIM THE UNIFORM.
I KNOW EVERYTHING AMUSES YOU, 'TASHA...BUT THIS ISN'T A JOKE.
I ASKED HIM TO SAVE BUCKY, CLINT.
THAT'S WHY TONY GAVE HIM THE MANTLE WHEN I WAS GONE.
AND I WASN'T GOING TO REVEAL THE MAN'S SECRETS...
THOSE ARE HIS DEMONS TO WRESTLE WITH.

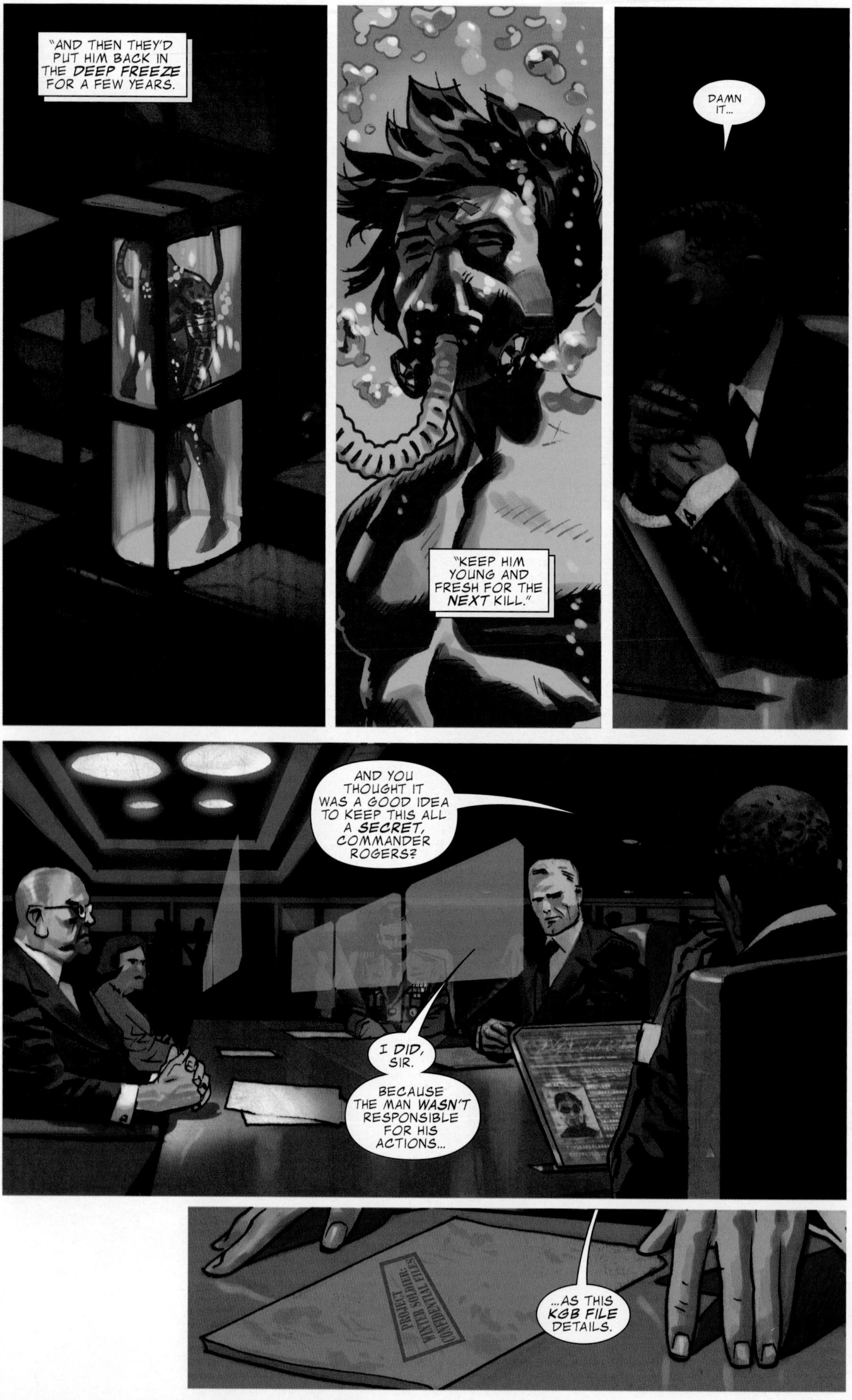
"AND THEN THEY'D PUT HIM BACK IN THE DEEP FREEZE FOR A FEW YEARS.
"KEEP HIM YOUNG AND FRESH FOR THE NEXT KILL."
DAMN IT...
AND YOU THOUGHT IT WAS A GOOD IDEA TO KEEP THIS ALL A SECRET, COMMANDER ROGERS?
I DID, SIR.
BECAUSE THE MAN WASN'T RESPONSIBLE FOR HIS ACTIONS...
...AS THIS KGB FILE DETAILS.
PROJECT WINTER SOLDIER: CONFIDENTIAL FILES

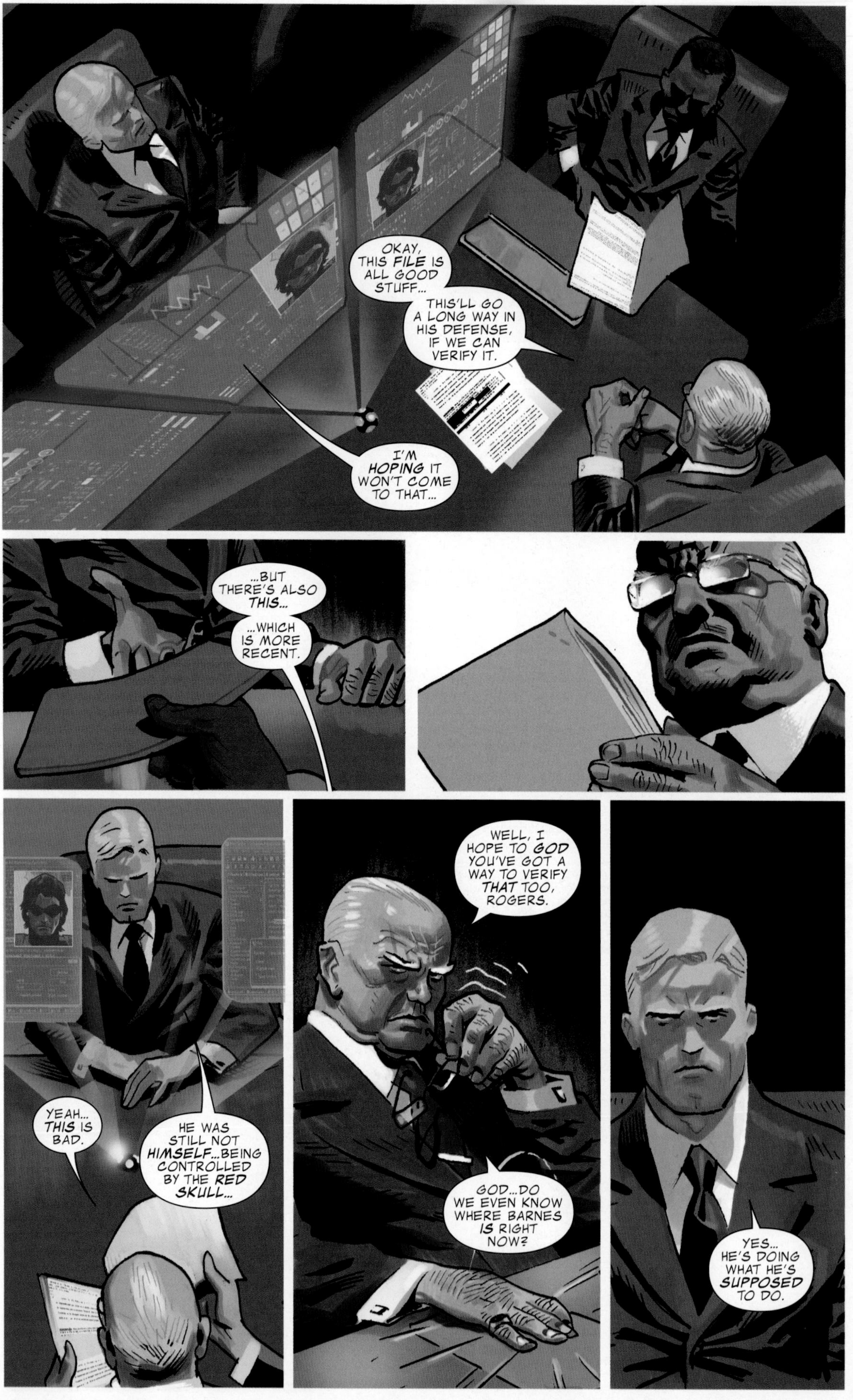
OKAY, THIS FILE IS ALL GOOD STUFF...
THIS'LL GO A LONG WAY IN HIS DEFENSE, IF WE CAN VERIFY IT.
I'M HOPING IT WON'T COME TO THAT...
...BUT THERE'S ALSO THIS...
...WHICH IS MORE RECENT.
YEAH... THIS IS BAD.
HE WAS STILL NOT HIMSELF...BEING CONTROLLED BY THE RED SKULL...
WELL, I HOPE TO GOD YOU'VE GOT A WAY TO VERIFY THAT TOO, ROGERS.
GOD...DO WE EVEN KNOW WHERE BARNES IS RIGHT NOW?
YES... HE'S DOING WHAT HE'S SUPPOSED TO DO.

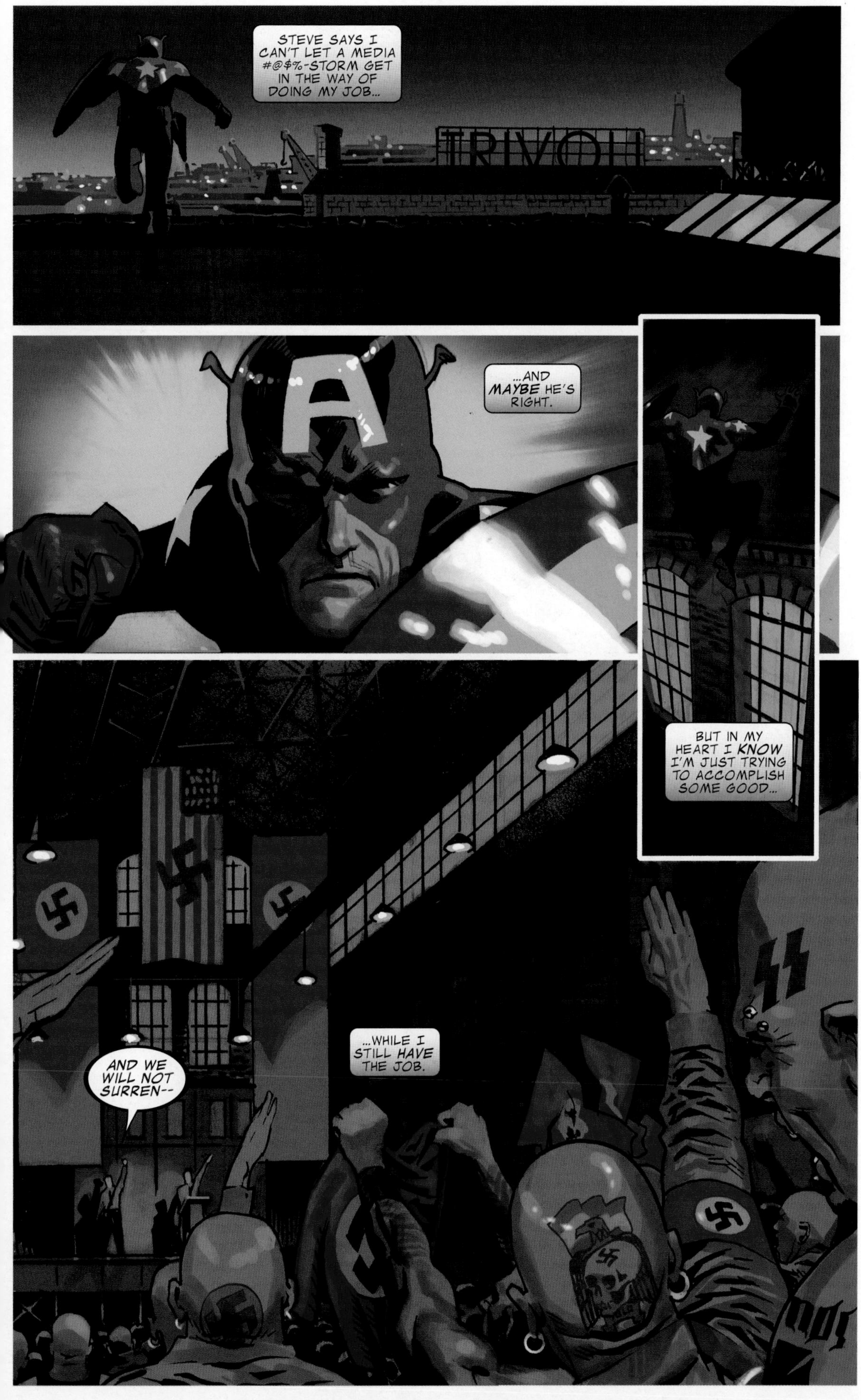
STEVE SAYS I CAN'T LET A MEDIA #@$%-STORM GET IN THE WAY OF DOING MY JOB...
TRIVOLI
...AND MAYBE HE'S RIGHT.
BUT IN MY HEART I KNOW I'M JUST TRYING TO ACCOMPLISH SOME GOOD...
AND WE WILL NOT SURREN--
...WHILE I STILL HAVE THE JOB.

SKRRASSH

BUT THERE'S ONE *OTHER* THING I KNOW...

--AAH!

KRAAAK

SORRY, FELLAS...

...TAKING OUT GUYS WEARING *SWASTIKAS* NEVER GETS OLD.

BLAM BLAM

...YOU PICKED THE *WRONG NIGHT* TO BE NAZIS IN NEW YORK!

KNNCH

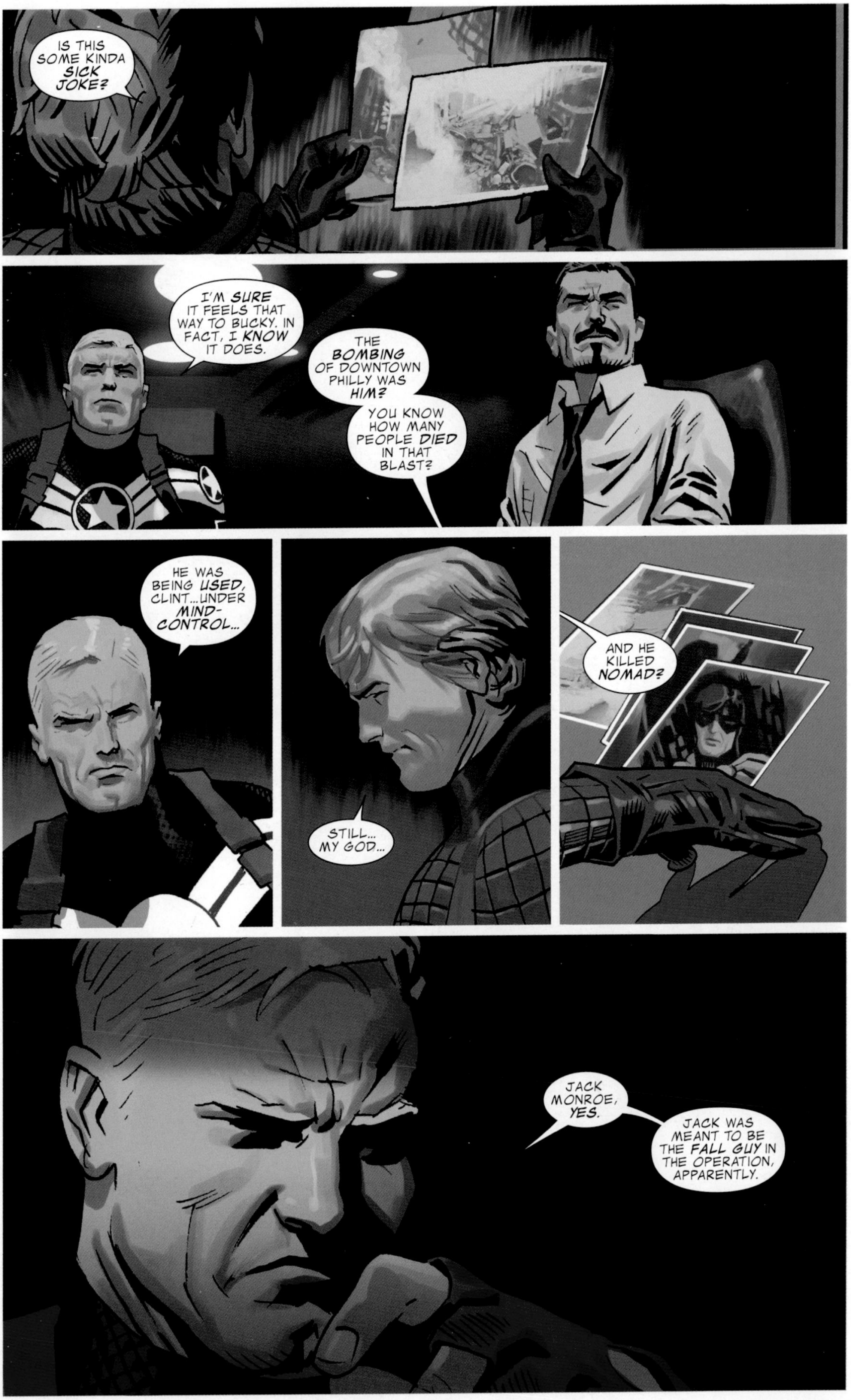
IS THIS SOME KINDA SICK JOKE?
I'M SURE IT FEELS THAT WAY TO BUCKY. IN FACT, I KNOW IT DOES.
THE BOMBING OF DOWNTOWN PHILLY WAS HIM?
YOU KNOW HOW MANY PEOPLE DIED IN THAT BLAST?
HE WAS BEING USED, CLINT...UNDER MIND-CONTROL...
STILL... MY GOD...
AND HE KILLED NOMAD?
JACK MONROE, YES.
JACK WAS MEANT TO BE THE FALL GUY IN THE OPERATION, APPARENTLY.

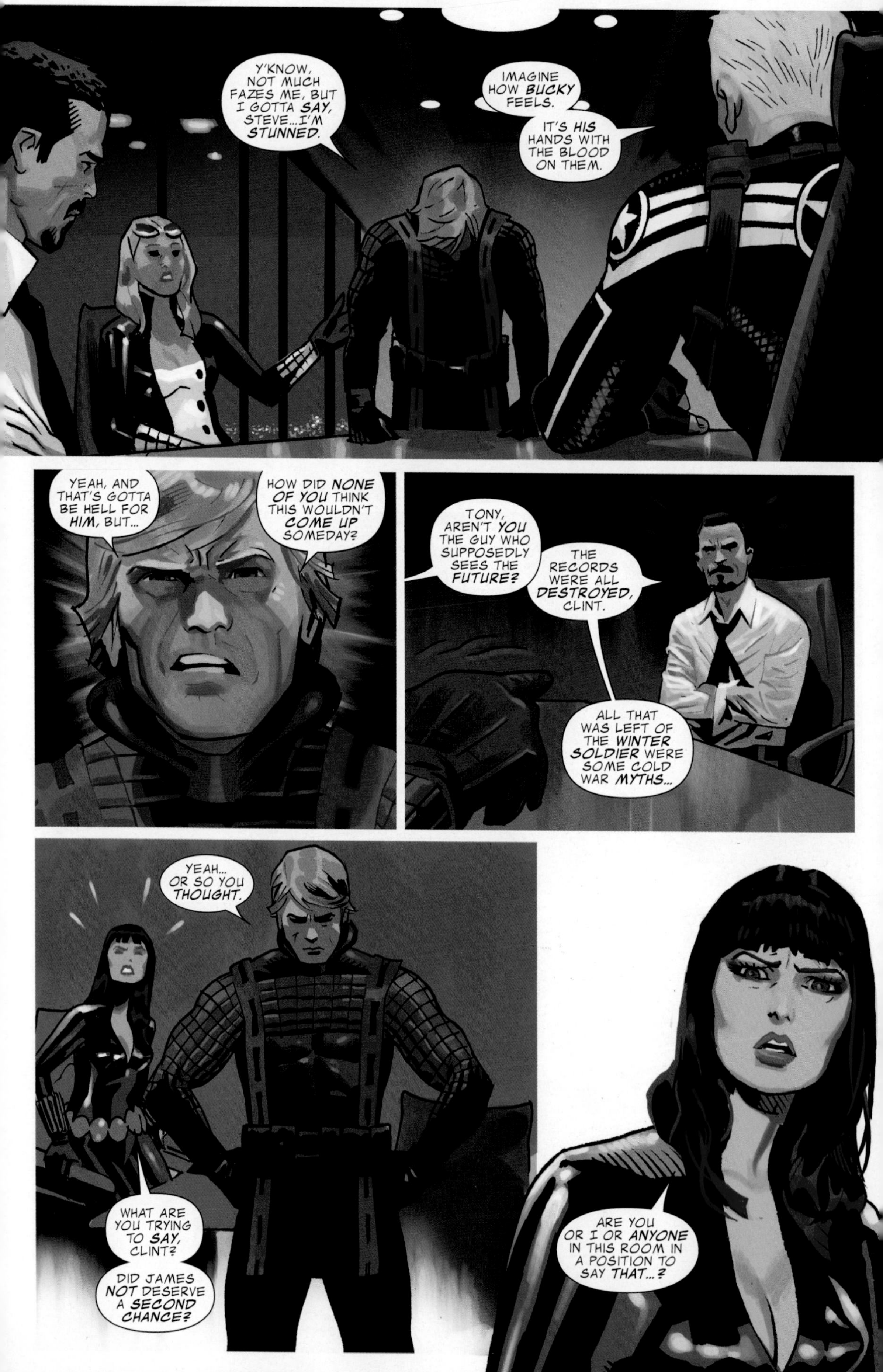
Y'KNOW, NOT MUCH FAZES ME, BUT I GOTTA SAY, STEVE...I'M STUNNED.
IMAGINE HOW BUCKY FEELS.
IT'S HIS HANDS WITH THE BLOOD ON THEM.
YEAH, AND THAT'S GOTTA BE HELL FOR HIM, BUT...
HOW DID NONE OF YOU THINK THIS WOULDN'T COME UP SOMEDAY?
TONY, AREN'T YOU THE GUY WHO SUPPOSEDLY SEES THE FUTURE?
THE RECORDS WERE ALL DESTROYED, CLINT.
ALL THAT WAS LEFT OF THE WINTER SOLDIER WERE SOME COLD WAR MYTHS...
YEAH... OR SO YOU THOUGHT.
WHAT ARE YOU TRYING TO SAY, CLINT?
DID JAMES NOT DESERVE A SECOND CHANCE?
ARE YOU OR I OR ANYONE IN THIS ROOM IN A POSITION TO SAY THAT...?

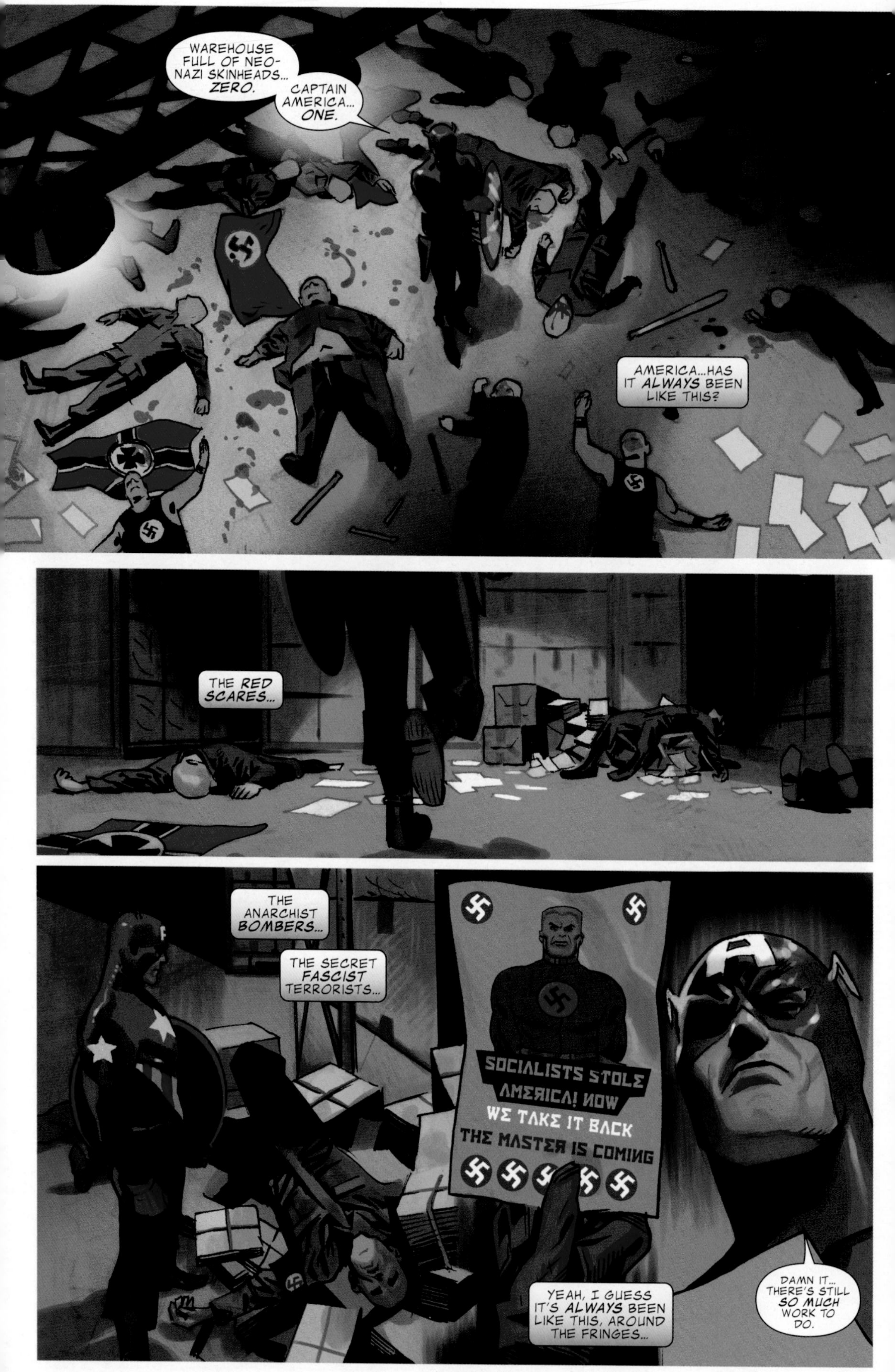
WAREHOUSE FULL OF NEO-NAZI SKINHEADS... ZERO.
CAPTAIN AMERICA... ONE.
AMERICA...HAS IT ALWAYS BEEN LIKE THIS?
THE RED SCARES...
THE ANARCHIST BOMBERS...
THE SECRET FASCIST TERRORISTS...
SOCIALISTS STOLE AMERICA! NOW WE TAKE IT BACK
THE MASTER IS COMING
YEAH, I GUESS IT'S ALWAYS BEEN LIKE THIS, AROUND THE FRINGES...
DAMN IT... THERE'S STILL SO MUCH WORK TO DO.

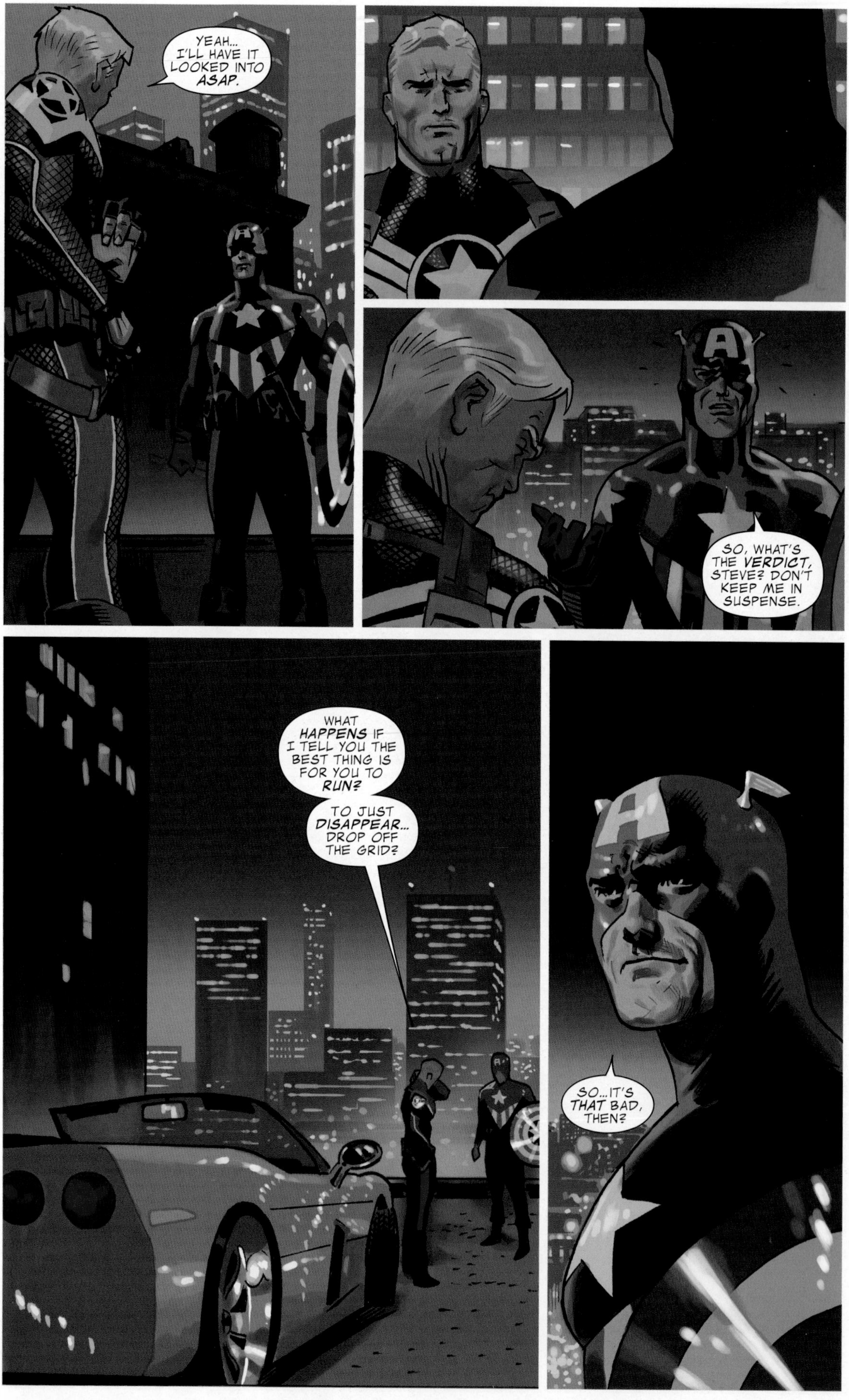
YEAH... I'LL HAVE IT LOOKED INTO *ASAP*.
SO, WHAT'S THE *VERDICT*, STEVE? DON'T KEEP ME IN SUSPENSE.
WHAT *HAPPENS* IF I TELL YOU THE BEST THING IS FOR YOU TO *RUN*?
TO JUST *DISAPPEAR*... DROP OFF THE GRID?
SO...IT'S *THAT* BAD, THEN?

BECAUSE IT'S NOT JUST ABOUT *YOU* ANYMORE...

IT'S ABOUT *POLITICS* AND PUBLIC OPINION AND THE *MEDIA* SPECTACLE...

AND YOU THINK THAT'S GONNA GET *BETTER* IF I *AMSCRAY*?

"NEW CAP DISAPPEARS" SOUNDS LIKE A STORY WITH SOME *LEGS* ON IT.

DAMN IT. IF I *EVER* SEE ZEMO AGAIN, I'M GONNA--

IT'S OKAY, STEVE.

THIS IS WHAT I *WANT*.

C'MON...IT'S TIME FOR ME TO *FACE THE PAST*...

NO MATTER WHAT.

YOU *DON'T*. I TOLD YOU, THIS IS GOING TO BE A *THREE RING CIRCUS*...

WELL, I GREW UP ON *MILITARY BASES*... I'VE NEVER *BEEN* TO THE CIRCUS, ACTUALLY.

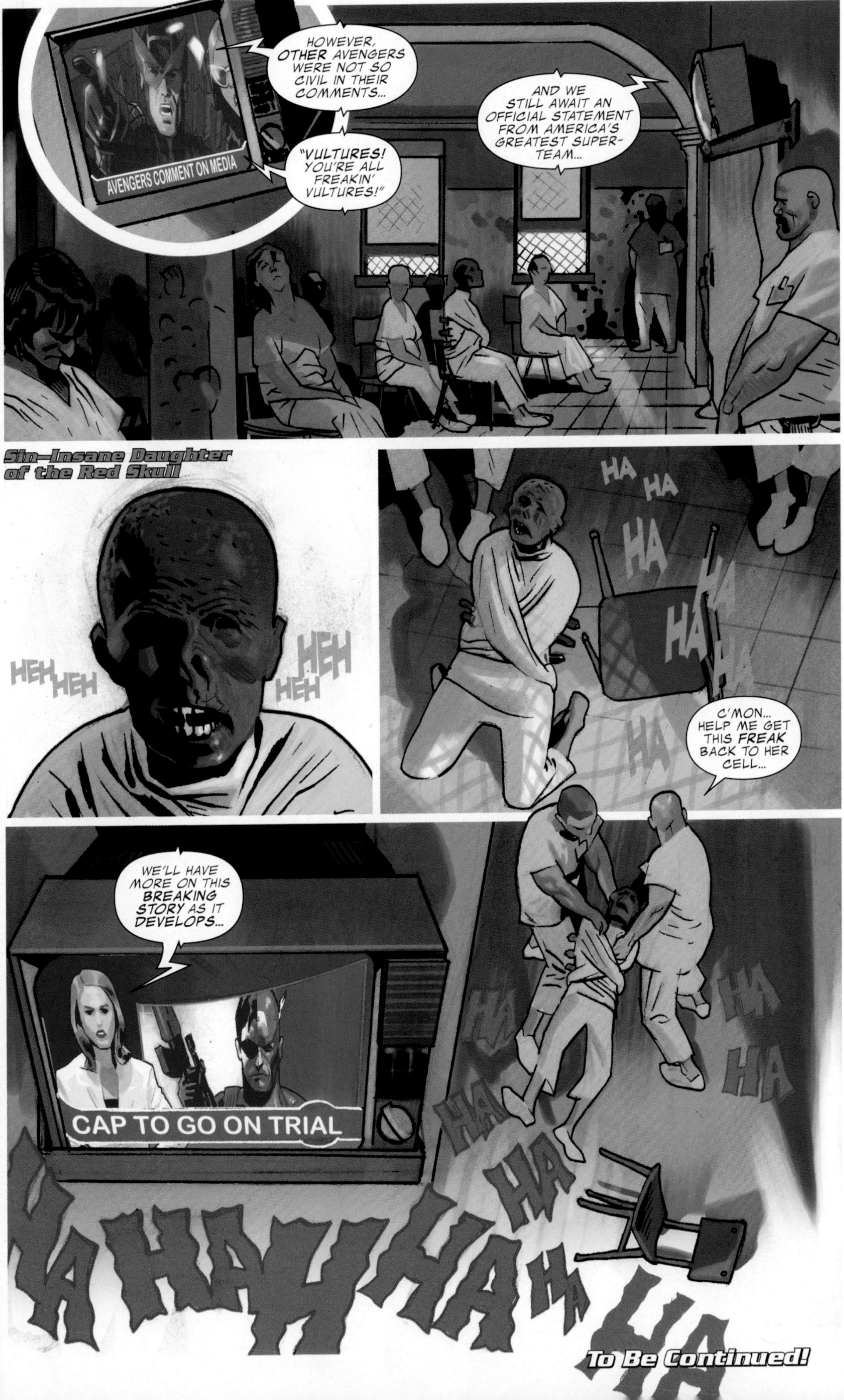
AVENGERS COMMENT ON MEDIA
HOWEVER, OTHER AVENGERS WERE NOT SO CIVIL IN THEIR COMMENTS...
"VULTURES! YOU'RE ALL FREAKIN' VULTURES!"
AND WE STILL AWAIT AN OFFICIAL STATEMENT FROM AMERICA'S GREATEST SUPER-TEAM...
Sin–Insane Daughter of the Red Skull
HEH HEH
HEH HEH HEH
HA HA HA HA HA HA HA HA
C'MON... HELP ME GET THIS FREAK BACK TO HER CELL...
WE'LL HAVE MORE ON THIS BREAKING STORY AS IT DEVELOPS...
CAP TO GO ON TRIAL
HA HA HA HA HA HA HA HA HA HA HA
To Be Continued!

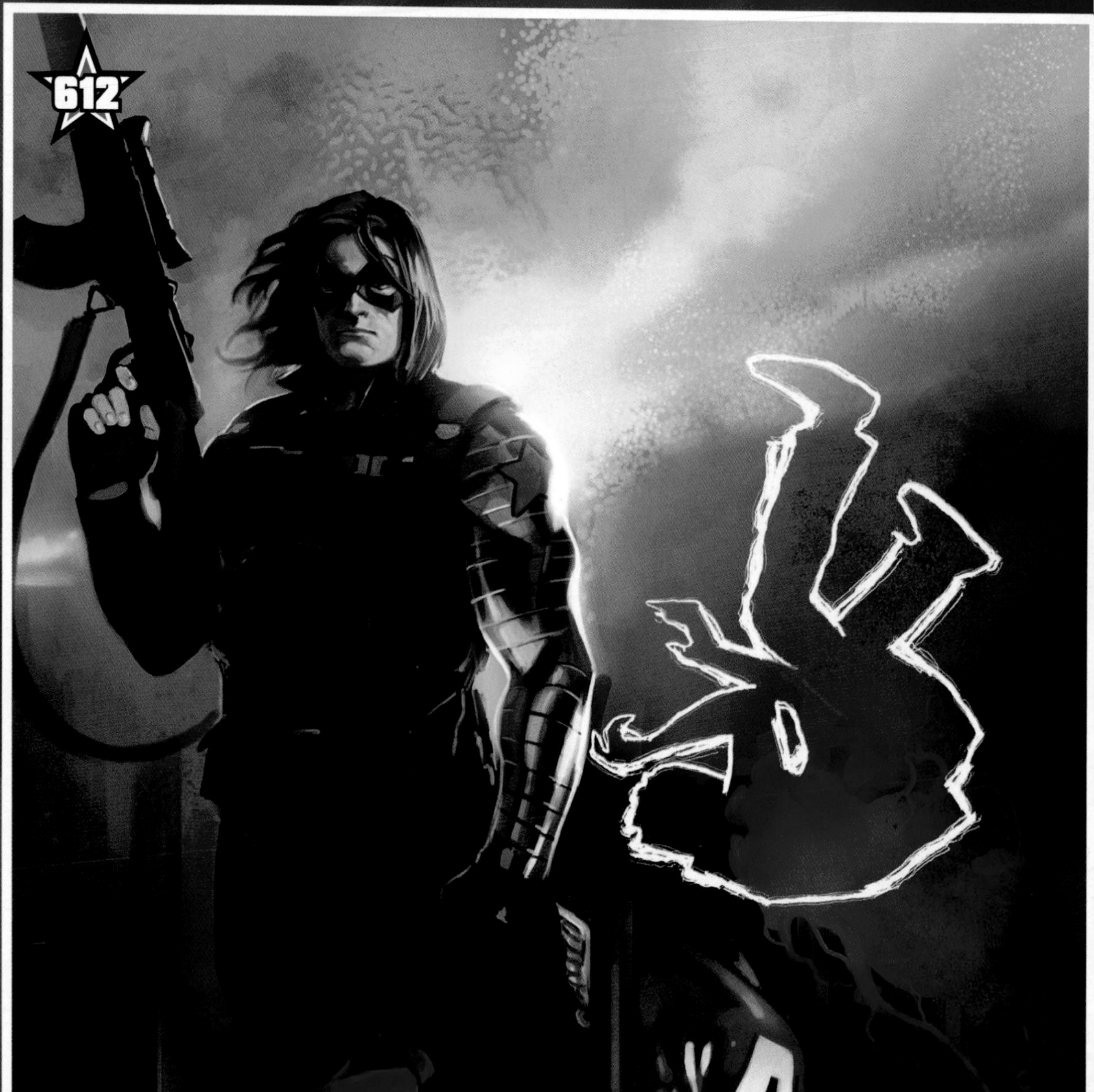
612

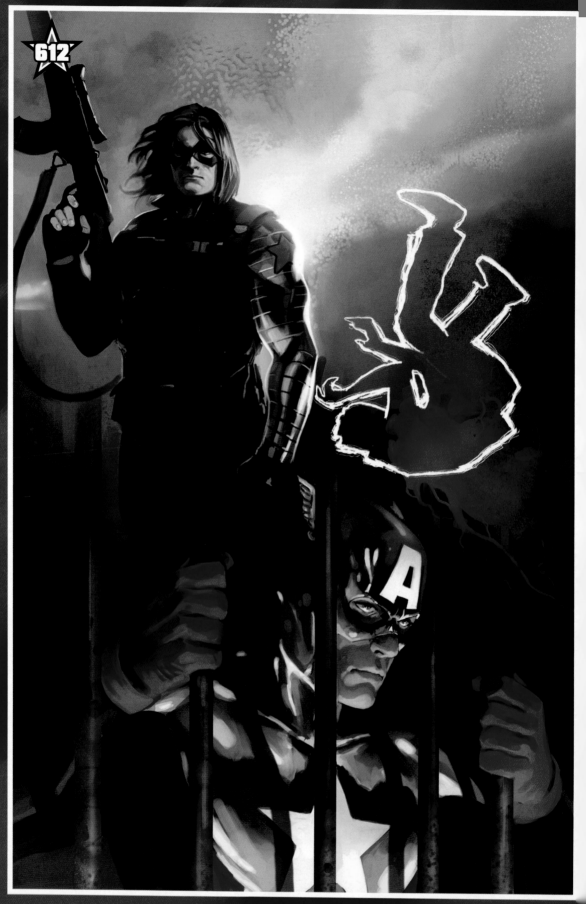

THE TRIAL OF CAPTAIN AMERICA PART 2

--IMPENDING TRIAL OF THE MAN WHO UNTIL RECENTLY WE KNEW ONLY AS CAPTAIN AMERICA.

100%

6:48 PM

**DAYS AWAY FROM JUSTICE, CAPTAIN AMERICA ON**

ONE-TIME BROTHER IN ARMS STEVE ROGERS, THE ORIGINAL CAP, STANDS BY HIS SIDE...

BUCKY BARNES IS A HERO... AND HE WILL BE EXONERATED OF ALL CHARGES.

**CAPTAIN AMERICA ON TRIAL**

...BUT AS THE WEEKS PASS, INFORMATION FROM ONCE-CLASSIFIED RUSSIAN DOCUMENTS CREATE A FRIGHTENING PICTURE OF BARNES' LIFE AS A SOVIET ASSASSIN...

CLASSIFI

100%

6:48 PM

**JUDGE DENIES BAIL FOR CAP**

...CAUSING A FEDERAL JUDGE TO DENY BAIL, AND INSTEAD FAST-TRACK...

POLICE G 9047

100%

6:48 PM

**NO SPECIAL TREATMENT FOR AVENGER**

...WHAT SOME ARE ALREADY CALLING THE TRIAL OF THE NEW CENTURY...

GOD, ENOUGH WITH THE ROUND-THE-CLOCK COVERAGE.

JUST PUT 'IM IN THE CHAIR ALREADY...

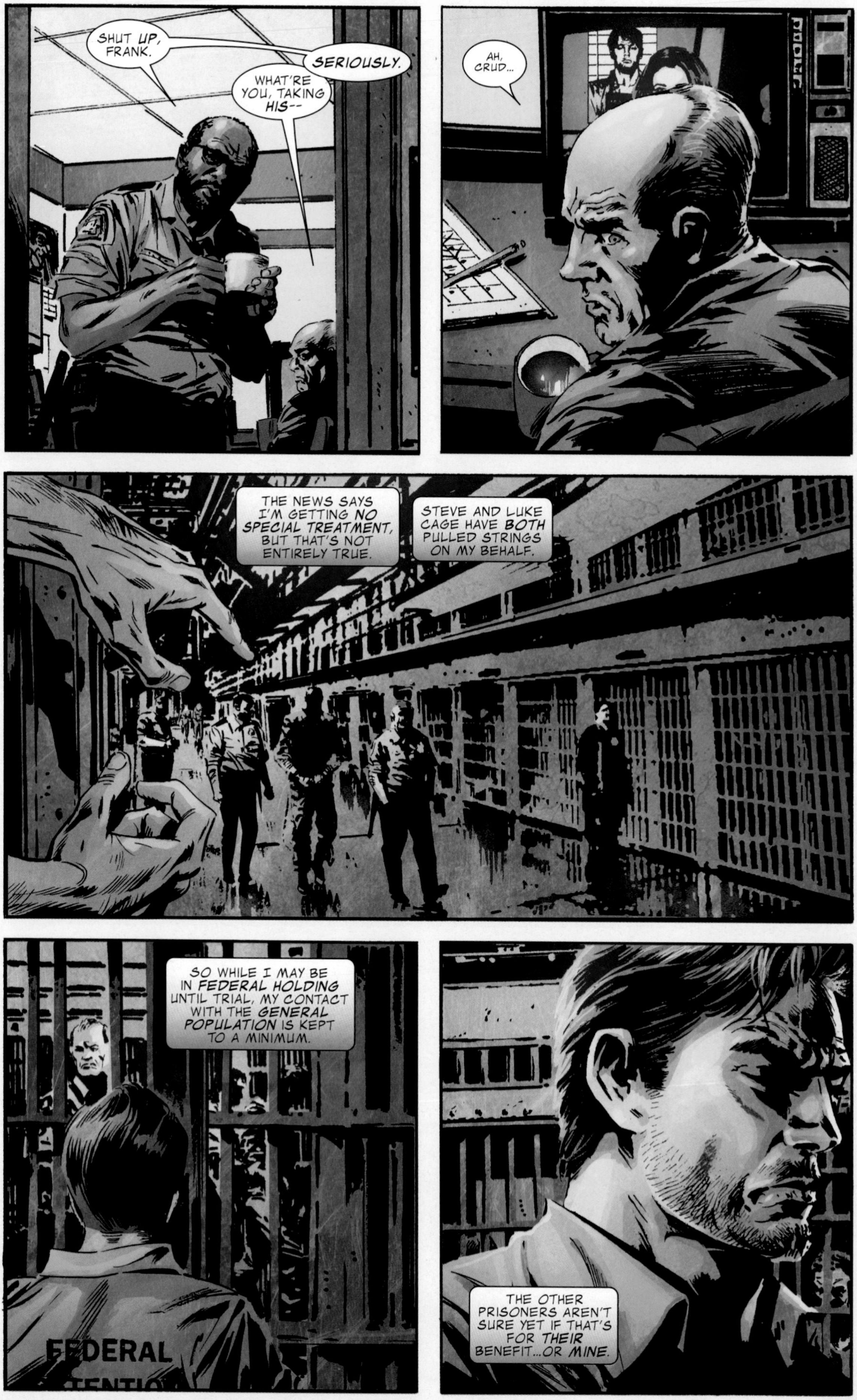
SHUT UP, FRANK.
SERIOUSLY.
WHAT'RE YOU, TAKING HIS--
AH, CRUD...
THE NEWS SAYS I'M GETTING NO SPECIAL TREATMENT, BUT THAT'S NOT ENTIRELY TRUE.
STEVE AND LUKE CAGE HAVE BOTH PULLED STRINGS ON MY BEHALF.
SO WHILE I MAY BE IN FEDERAL HOLDING UNTIL TRIAL, MY CONTACT WITH THE GENERAL POPULATION IS KEPT TO A MINIMUM.
FEDERAL
THE OTHER PRISONERS AREN'T SURE YET IF THAT'S FOR THEIR BENEFIT...OR MINE.

AND I WAS ALLOWED TO KEEP MY CYBERNETIC *LEFT ARM*, AFTER TONY STARK *MODIFIED* IT TO BE *NO STRONGER* THAN A NORMAL ARM.

FEDERAL DETENTION

NOW IT'S JUST A *PROSTHETIC*, ACCORDING TO THE LAW.

THAT TOOK *DAYS* TO GET USED TO.

*TRAPPED BEHIND BARS...WEAKER* THAN I'VE FELT IN YEARS...

IF *THIS* IS MY PATH TO REDEMPTION, I'M SURE AS HELL *EARNING* IT.

OKAY, *PRISONER...* THIRTY MINUTES...

OH GOOD, FINALLY...

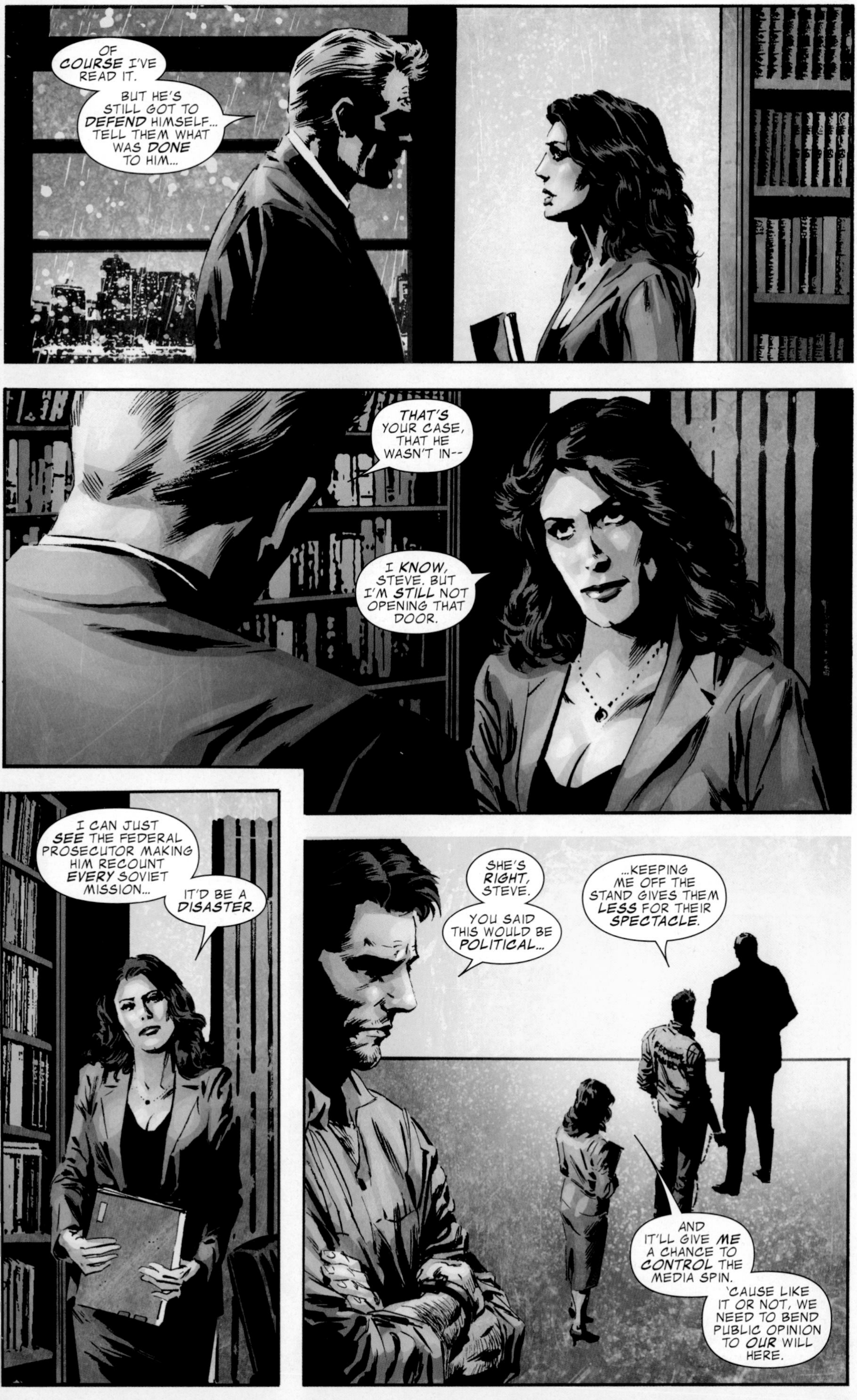

OF COURSE I'VE READ IT.
BUT HE'S STILL GOT TO DEFEND HIMSELF... TELL THEM WHAT WAS DONE TO HIM...
THAT'S YOUR CASE, THAT HE WASN'T IN--
I KNOW, STEVE. BUT I'M STILL NOT OPENING THAT DOOR.
I CAN JUST SEE THE FEDERAL PROSECUTOR MAKING HIM RECOUNT EVERY SOVIET MISSION...
IT'D BE A DISASTER.
SHE'S RIGHT, STEVE.
YOU SAID THIS WOULD BE POLITICAL...
...KEEPING ME OFF THE STAND GIVES THEM LESS FOR THEIR SPECTACLE.
AND IT'LL GIVE ME A CHANCE TO CONTROL THE MEDIA SPIN.
'CAUSE LIKE IT OR NOT, WE NEED TO BEND PUBLIC OPINION TO OUR WILL HERE.

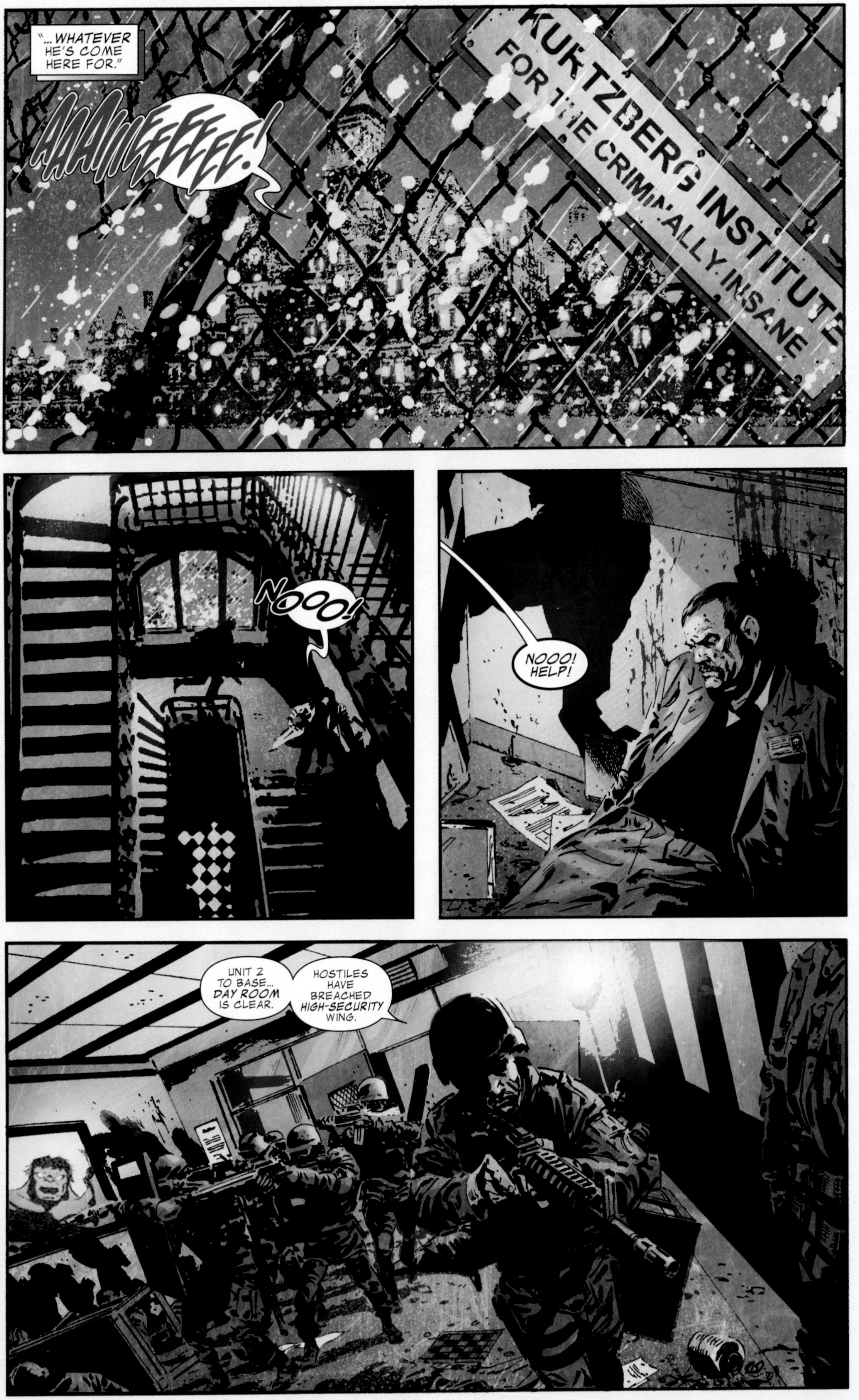
"...WHATEVER HE'S COME HERE FOR."
AAAAIIIEEEEEE!
KURTZBERG INSTITUTE FOR THE CRIMINALLY INSANE
NOOO!
NOOO! HELP!
UNIT 2 TO BASE... DAY ROOM IS CLEAR.
HOSTILES HAVE BREACHED HIGH-SECURITY WING.

PREPARING TO ENGAGE.

KA-BLAAM
BLAAM

SUCK ON THIS, COP!

BRATATATATATAT

AHHH!

BLAAM
BLAAM

IDIOTS... STOP PLAYING WITH THEM...

GAAH!

RATATATATATA

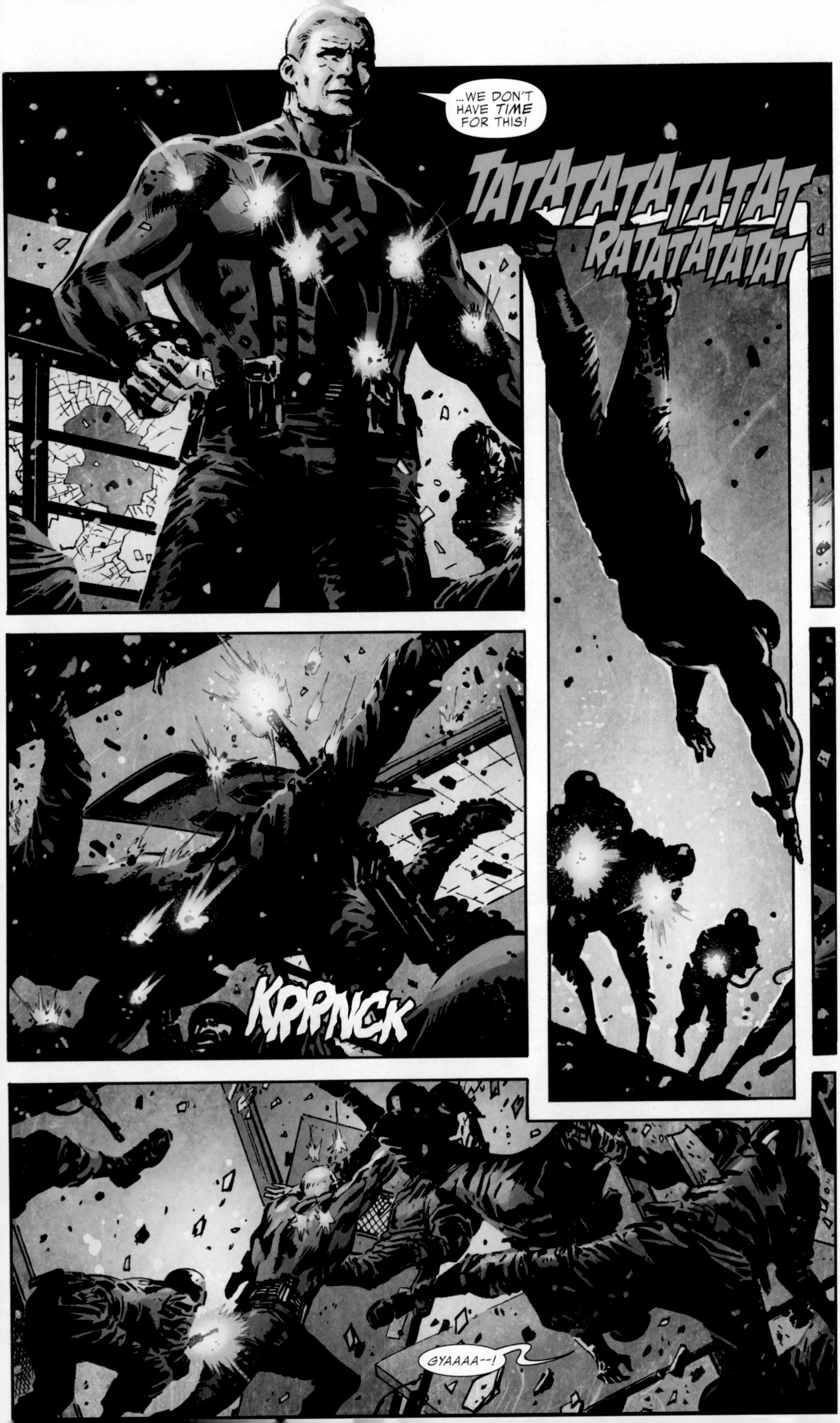
...WE DON'T HAVE TIME FOR THIS!
TATATATATATAT
RATATATATAT
KPRNCK
GYAAAA--!

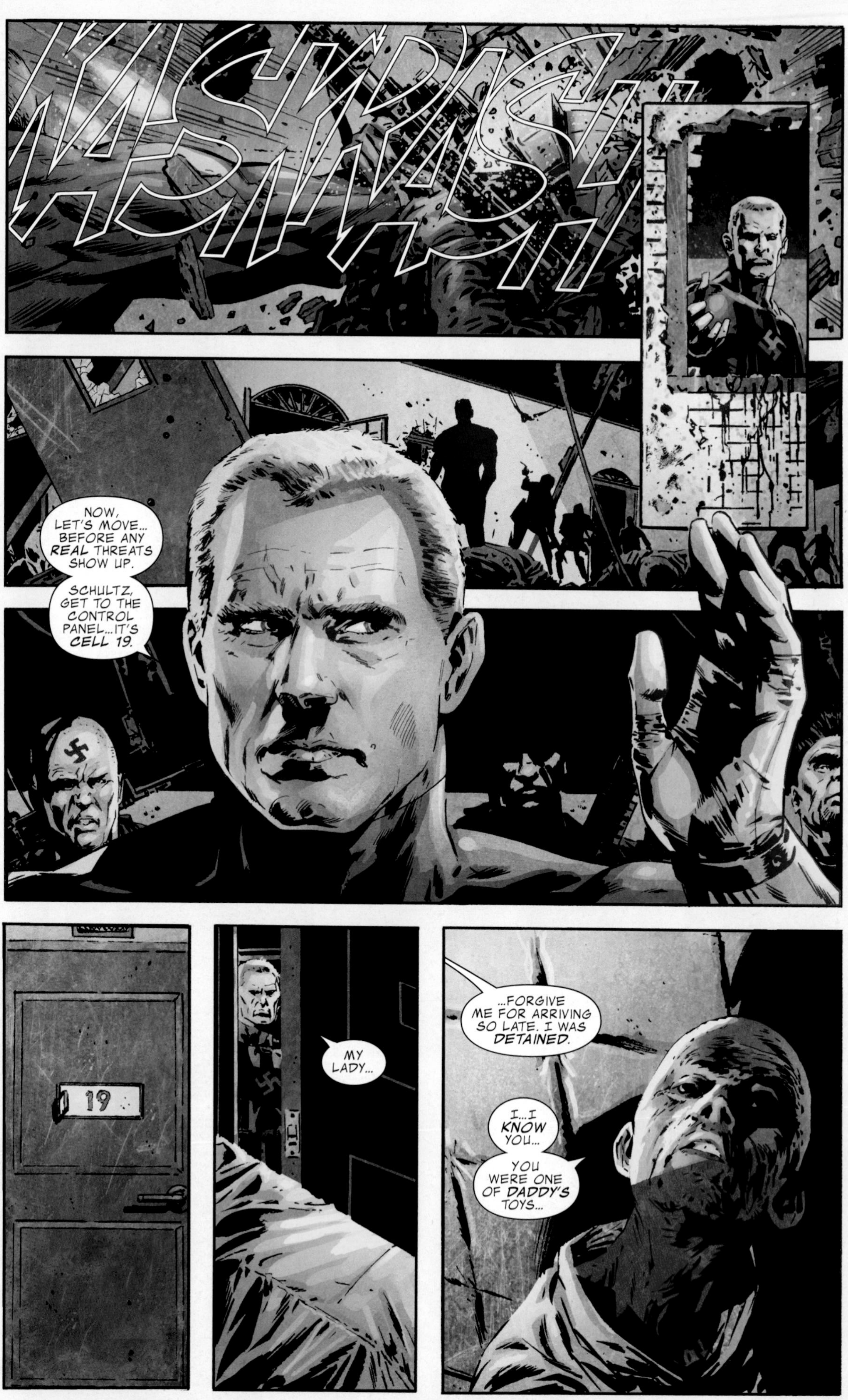
NOW, LET'S MOVE... BEFORE ANY REAL THREATS SHOW UP.
SCHULTZ, GET TO THE CONTROL PANEL...IT'S CELL 19.
19
MY LADY...
...FORGIVE ME FOR ARRIVING SO LATE. I WAS DETAINED.
I...I KNOW YOU...
YOU WERE ONE OF DADDY'S TOYS...

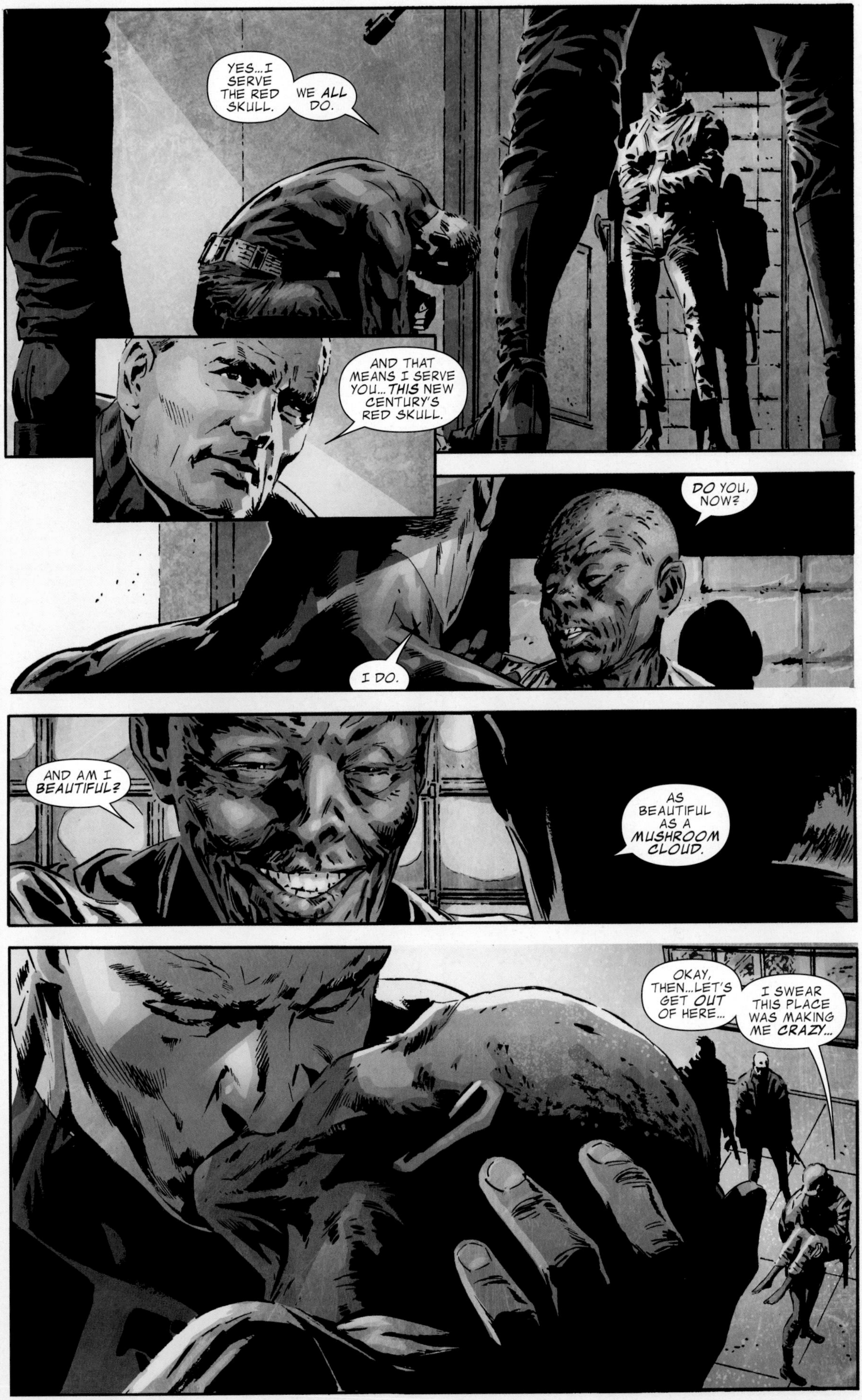
YES...I SERVE THE RED SKULL.
WE ALL DO.
AND THAT MEANS I SERVE YOU... THIS NEW CENTURY'S RED SKULL.
DO YOU, NOW?
I DO.
AND AM I BEAUTIFUL?
AS BEAUTIFUL AS A MUSHROOM CLOUD.
OKAY, THEN...LET'S GET OUT OF HERE...
I SWEAR THIS PLACE WAS MAKING ME CRAZY...

SO, WHAT DO YOU REALLY THINK, BERNIE...?

I THINK I DON'T KNOW...

I MEAN, I'M LOOKING TO AVOID *WORST CASE* SCENARIOS...

LIKE YOUR *OLDEST FRIEND* SPENDING TWENTY YEARS IN SOLITARY.

BUT I'M WORRYING THAT MIGHT NOT BE *GOOD ENOUGH* FOR THE TWO OF YOU.

WHAT DO YOU *MEAN?*

OUR *ENTIRE DEFENSE* RESTS ON PROVING BUCKY WAS UNDER *MIND-CONTROL.*

AND THAT'S *JUST* TO GET TO *REASONABLE DOUBT.*

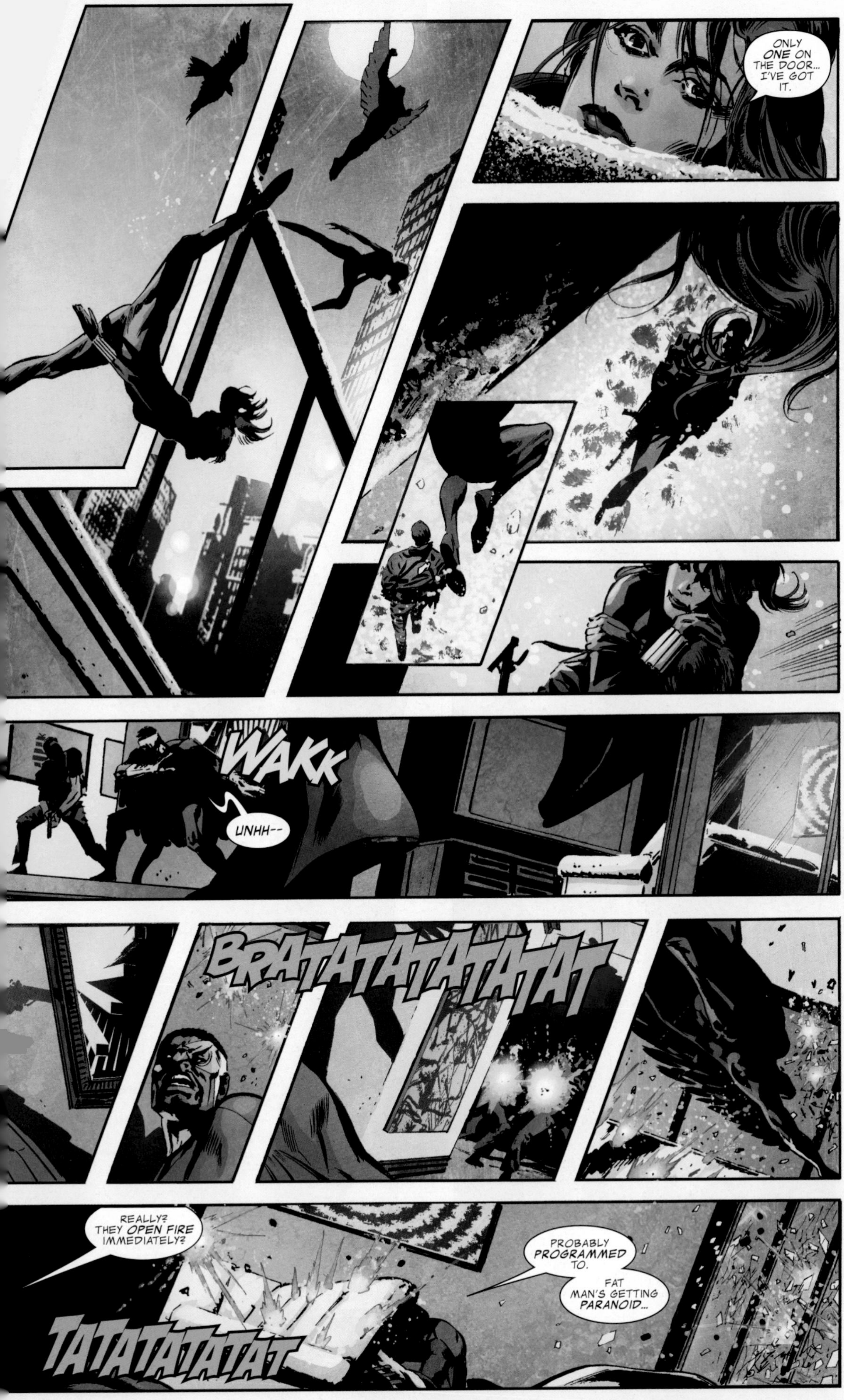
ONLY ONE ON THE DOOR... I'VE GOT IT.
WAKK
UNHH--
BRATATATATATATAT
REALLY? THEY OPEN FIRE IMMEDIATELY?
PROBABLY PROGRAMMED TO.
FAT MAN'S GETTING PARANOID...
TATATATATAT

DON'T LISTEN. HIS VOICE IS HIS TRICK...

OH, COME ON...I'M COOPERATING.

I'M EVEN WILLING TO MAKE A DEAL.

I'VE SEEN THE NEWS, AFTER ALL...

IT SEEMS LIKE YOU'RE GOING TO NEED ME...DOESN'T IT?

7 DAY FORECAST
THU  FRI  SAT  SUN
30%  41  46  
42  28  24
25

KRAAK

I SAID, SHUT UP!

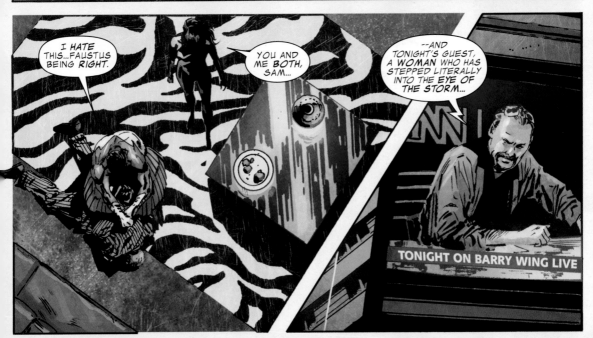

I HATE THIS...FAUSTUS BEING RIGHT.

YOU AND ME BOTH, SAM...

--AND TONIGHT'S GUEST, A WOMAN WHO HAS STEPPED LITERALLY INTO THE EYE OF THE STORM...

TONIGHT ON BARRY WING LIVE

THE *NOISE* IN PRISON IS INSANE.

ECHOED SCREAMING...

CLANGING BARS...

FIGHTS...

THREATS YELLED BETWEEN CELLS...

IT'S *NOT* LIKE A MILITARY BRIG.

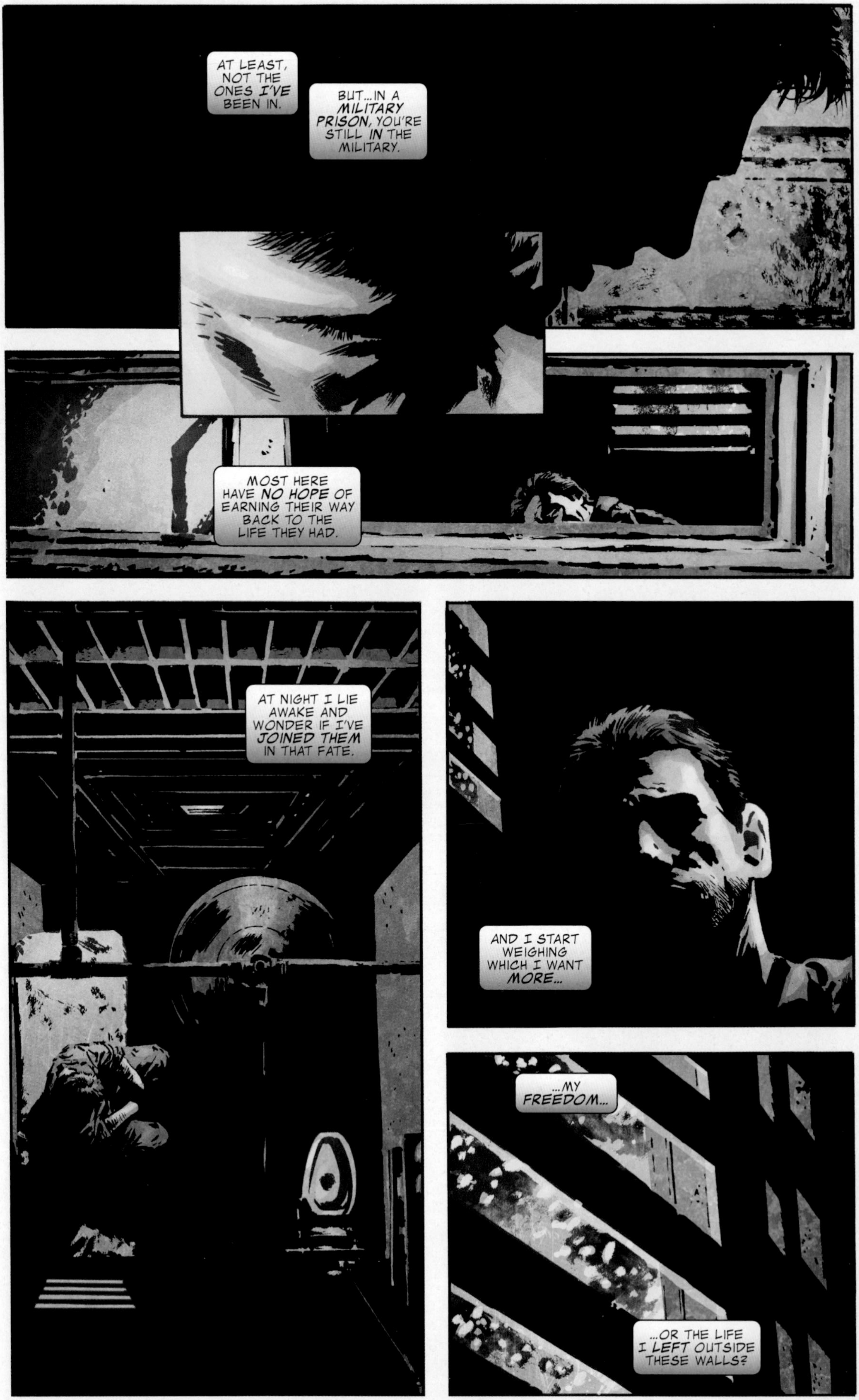
AT LEAST, NOT THE ONES I'VE BEEN IN.
BUT...IN A MILITARY PRISON, YOU'RE STILL IN THE MILITARY.
MOST HERE HAVE NO HOPE OF EARNING THEIR WAY BACK TO THE LIFE THEY HAD.
AT NIGHT I LIE AWAKE AND WONDER IF I'VE JOINED THEM IN THAT FATE.
AND I START WEIGHING WHICH I WANT MORE...
...MY FREEDOM...
...OR THE LIFE I LEFT OUTSIDE THESE WALLS?

I NEVER *ASKED*-- NEVER *WANTED*-- TO BE CAPTAIN AMERICA...

BUT THAT MASK, THOSE STARS AND STRIPES, THAT SHIELD...

...THEY *CHANGE* YOU.

I CAN SEE NOW THE *BURDEN* THAT STEVE'S *ALWAYS* CARRIED.

AND IT FEELS STRANGE TO ADMIT I WANT THAT BURDEN BACK...

BUT UNDERNEATH IT ALL, WHAT I *REALLY* KNOW IS...

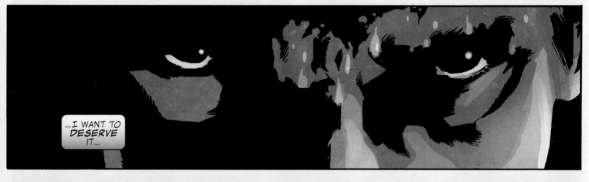

...I WANT TO *DESERVE* IT...

...SOMEHOW.

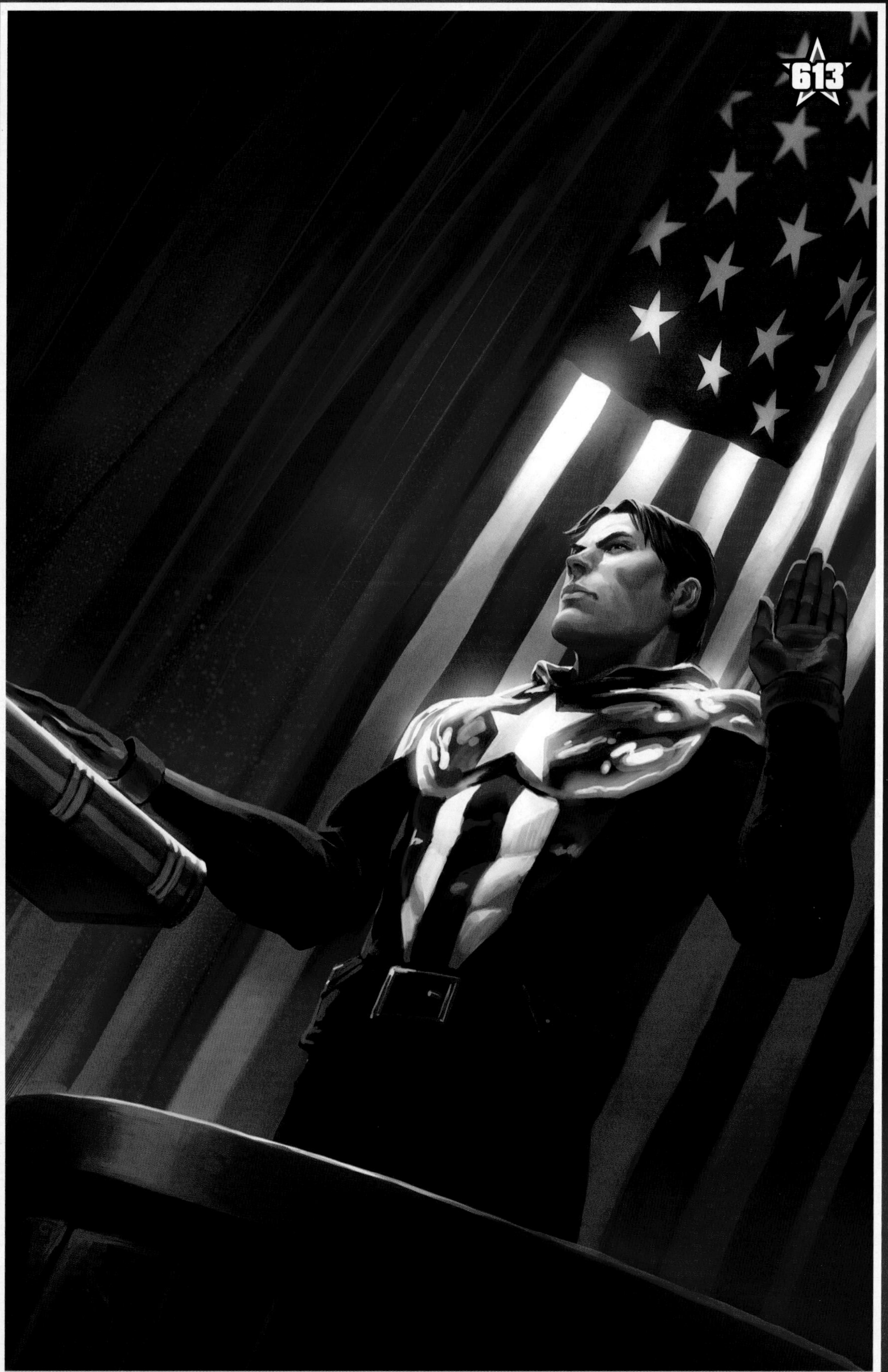
613

THE TRIAL OF CAPTAIN AMERICA PART 3

SORRY, AUTHORIZED PERSONNEL ONLY PAST THIS POINT...

WE'RE AS AUTHORIZED AS IT *GETS*, SON. *AVENGERS* SECURITY CLEARANCE.

YOUR CAPTAIN IS *EXPECTING* US.

OH, UH...YES, MA'AM...

THE CAPTAIN'S RIGHT DOWN THAT WAY... ...IN THE SECURITY BOOTH.

CRIME SCENE DO NOT CROSS

CRIME SCENE DO NO

WOW... AVENGERS...

I KNEW THIS WAS *BIG*...BUT I THOUGHT LIKE JUST *FBI* BIG...

YEAH...

WONDER WHO *ESCAPED* FROM THIS HELLHOLE?

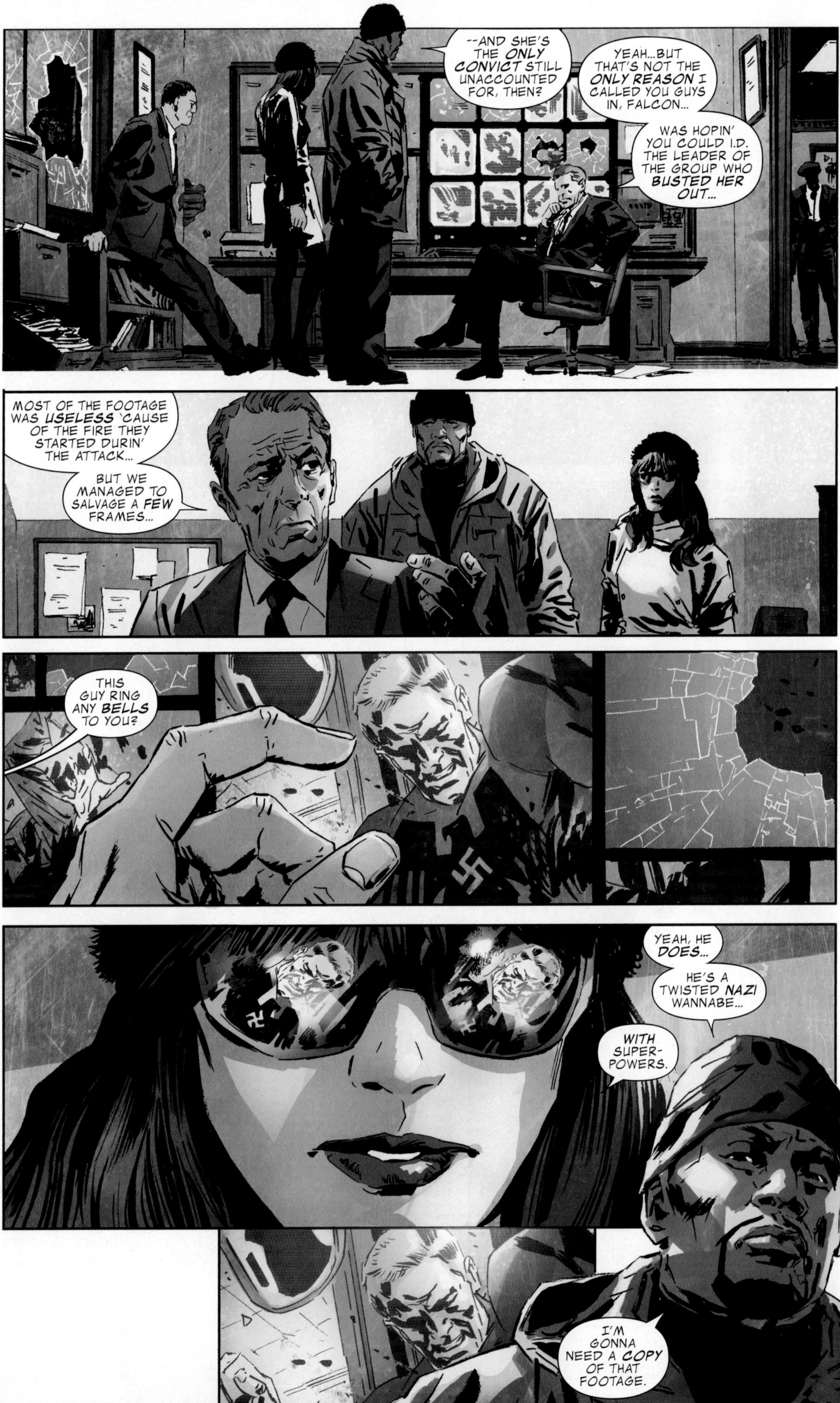
--AND SHE'S THE ONLY CONVICT STILL UNACCOUNTED FOR, THEN?
YEAH...BUT THAT'S NOT THE ONLY REASON I CALLED YOU GUYS IN, FALCON...
WAS HOPIN' YOU COULD I.D. THE LEADER OF THE GROUP WHO BUSTED HER OUT...
MOST OF THE FOOTAGE WAS USELESS 'CAUSE OF THE FIRE THEY STARTED DURIN' THE ATTACK...
BUT WE MANAGED TO SALVAGE A FEW FRAMES...
THIS GUY RING ANY BELLS TO YOU?
YEAH, HE DOES...
HE'S A TWISTED NAZI WANNABE...
WITH SUPER-POWERS.
I'M GONNA NEED A COPY OF THAT FOOTAGE.

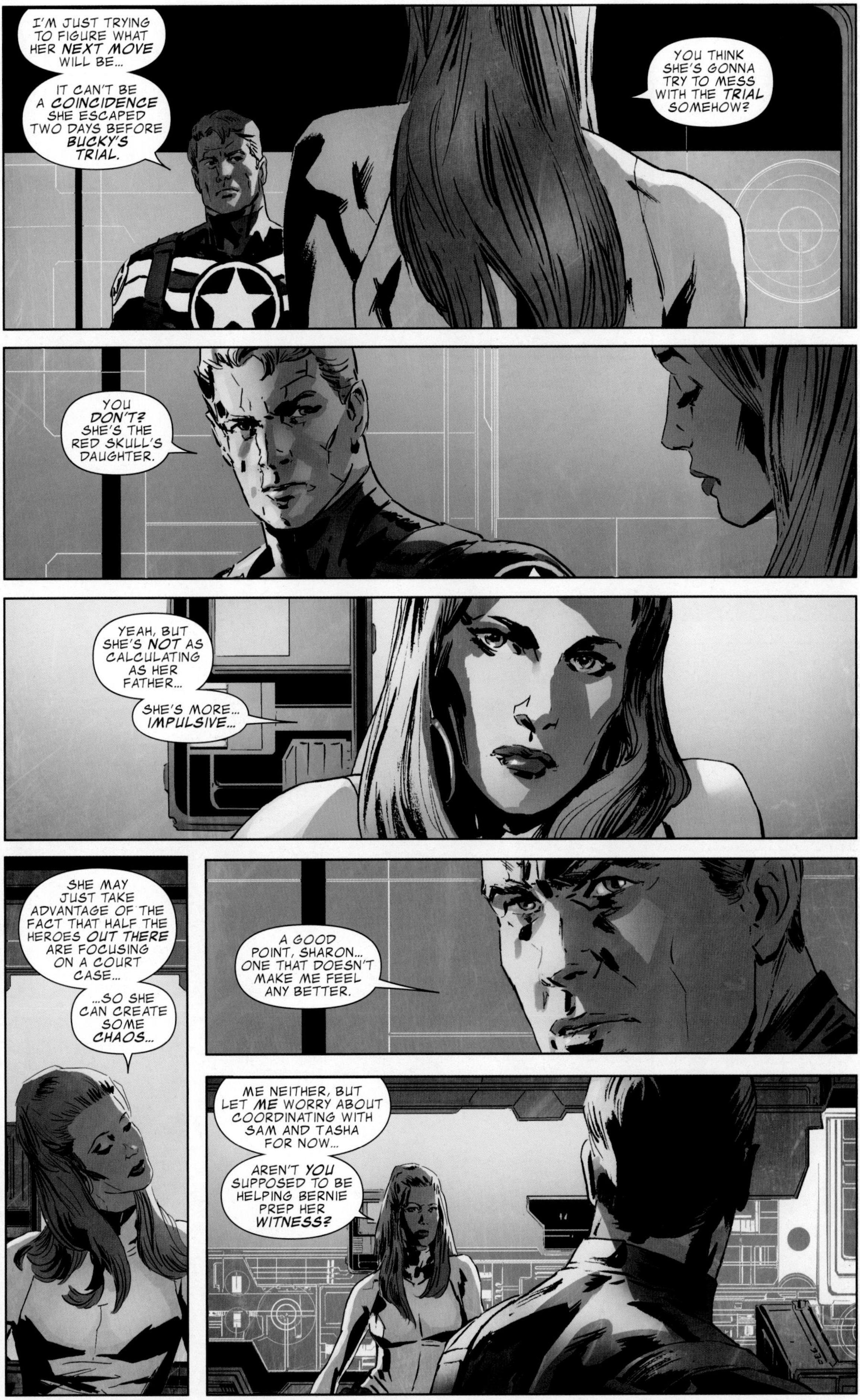
I'M JUST TRYING TO FIGURE WHAT HER NEXT MOVE WILL BE...
IT CAN'T BE A COINCIDENCE SHE ESCAPED TWO DAYS BEFORE BUCKY'S TRIAL.
YOU THINK SHE'S GONNA TRY TO MESS WITH THE TRIAL SOMEHOW?
YOU DON'T? SHE'S THE RED SKULL'S DAUGHTER.
YEAH, BUT SHE'S NOT AS CALCULATING AS HER FATHER...
SHE'S MORE... IMPULSIVE...
SHE MAY JUST TAKE ADVANTAGE OF THE FACT THAT HALF THE HEROES OUT THERE ARE FOCUSING ON A COURT CASE...
...SO SHE CAN CREATE SOME CHAOS...
A GOOD POINT, SHARON... ONE THAT DOESN'T MAKE ME FEEL ANY BETTER.
ME NEITHER, BUT LET ME WORRY ABOUT COORDINATING WITH SAM AND TASHA FOR NOW...
AREN'T YOU SUPPOSED TO BE HELPING BERNIE PREP HER WITNESS?

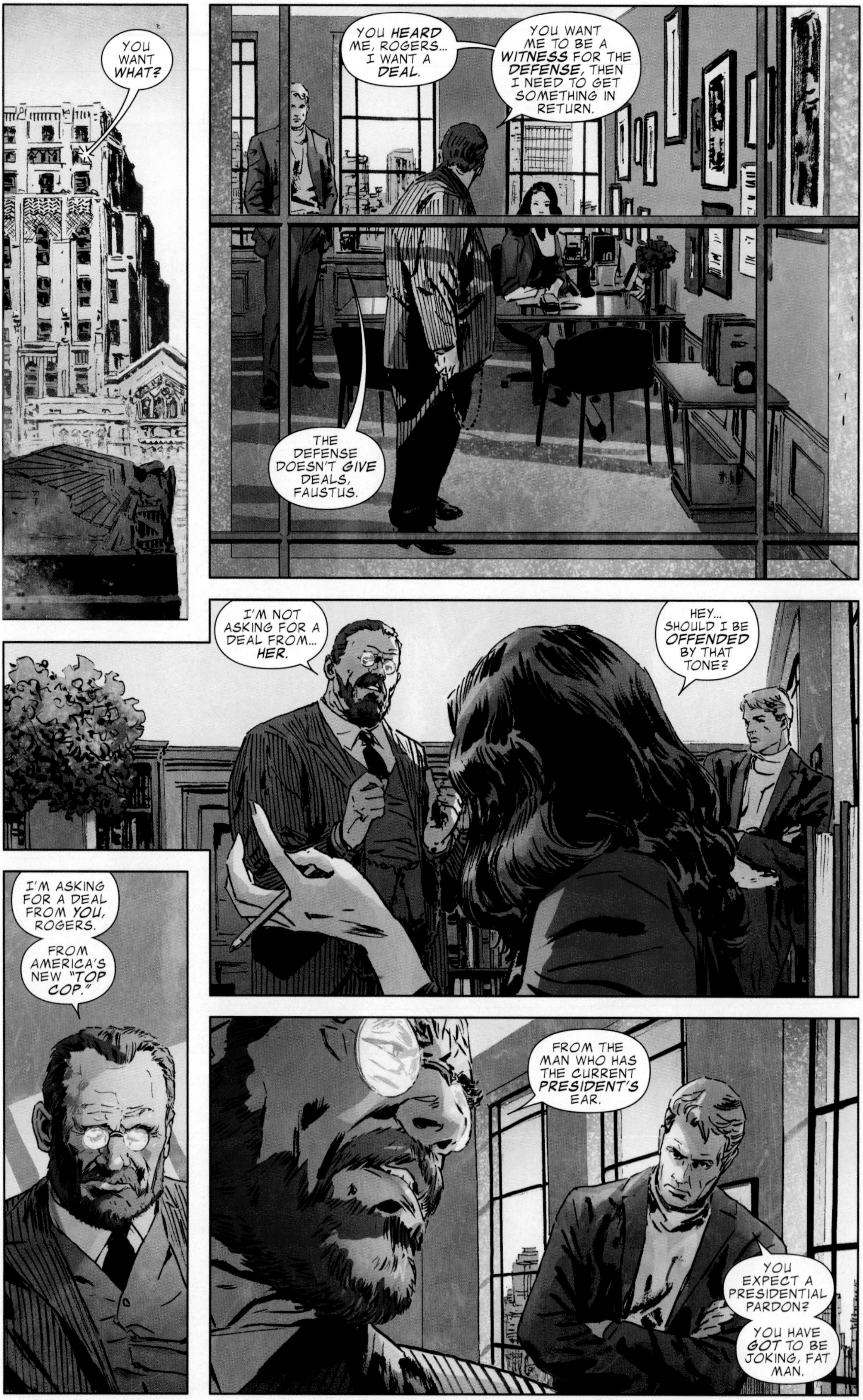
YOU WANT WHAT?
YOU HEARD ME, ROGERS... I WANT A DEAL.
YOU WANT ME TO BE A WITNESS FOR THE DEFENSE, THEN I NEED TO GET SOMETHING IN RETURN.
THE DEFENSE DOESN'T GIVE DEALS, FAUSTUS.
I'M NOT ASKING FOR A DEAL FROM... HER.
HEY... SHOULD I BE OFFENDED BY THAT TONE?
I'M ASKING FOR A DEAL FROM YOU, ROGERS.
FROM AMERICA'S NEW "TOP COP."
FROM THE MAN WHO HAS THE CURRENT PRESIDENT'S EAR.
YOU EXPECT A PRESIDENTIAL PARDON?
YOU HAVE GOT TO BE JOKING, FAT MAN.

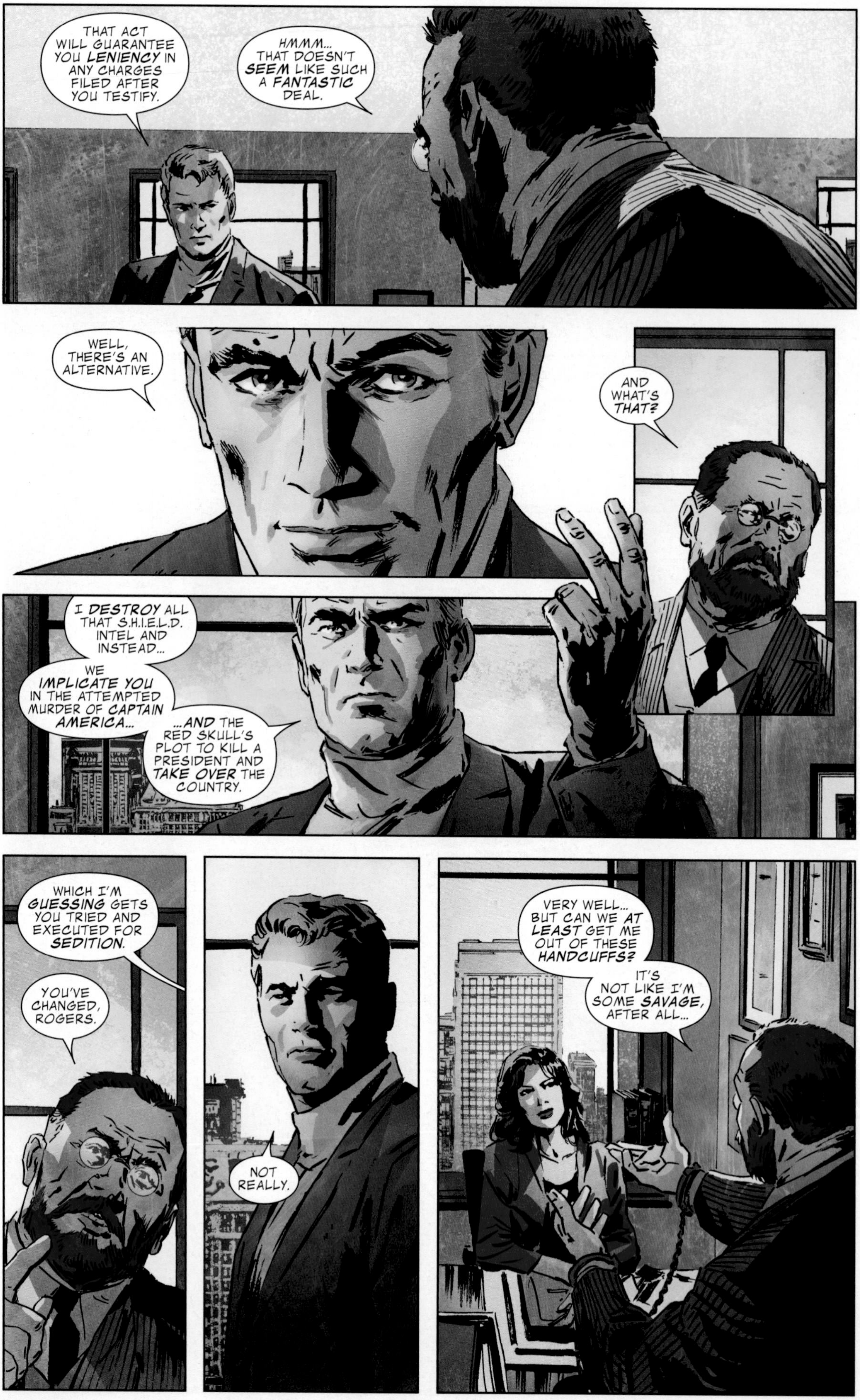
THAT ACT WILL GUARANTEE YOU LENIENCY IN ANY CHARGES FILED AFTER YOU TESTIFY.
HMMM... THAT DOESN'T SEEM LIKE SUCH A FANTASTIC DEAL.
WELL, THERE'S AN ALTERNATIVE.
AND WHAT'S THAT?
I DESTROY ALL THAT S.H.I.E.L.D. INTEL AND INSTEAD...
WE IMPLICATE YOU IN THE ATTEMPTED MURDER OF CAPTAIN AMERICA...
...AND THE RED SKULL'S PLOT TO KILL A PRESIDENT AND TAKE OVER THE COUNTRY.
WHICH I'M GUESSING GETS YOU TRIED AND EXECUTED FOR SEDITION.
YOU'VE CHANGED, ROGERS.
NOT REALLY.
VERY WELL... BUT CAN WE AT LEAST GET ME OUT OF THESE HANDCUFFS?
IT'S NOT LIKE I'M SOME SAVAGE, AFTER ALL...

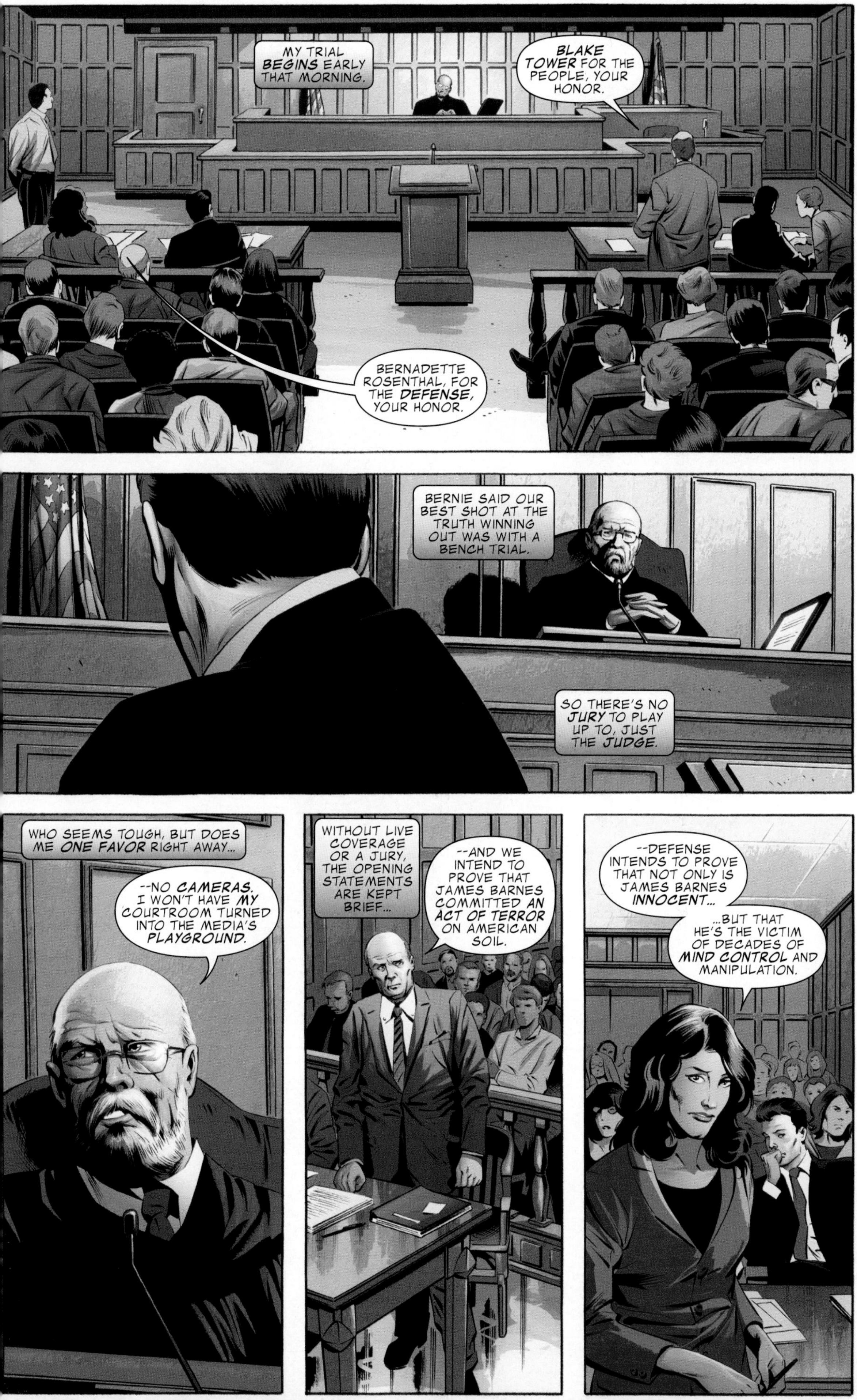
MY TRIAL BEGINS EARLY THAT MORNING.
BLAKE TOWER FOR THE PEOPLE, YOUR HONOR.
BERNADETTE ROSENTHAL, FOR THE DEFENSE, YOUR HONOR.
BERNIE SAID OUR BEST SHOT AT THE TRUTH WINNING OUT WAS WITH A BENCH TRIAL.
SO THERE'S NO JURY TO PLAY UP TO, JUST THE JUDGE.
WHO SEEMS TOUGH, BUT DOES ME ONE FAVOR RIGHT AWAY...
--NO CAMERAS. I WON'T HAVE MY COURTROOM TURNED INTO THE MEDIA'S PLAYGROUND.
WITHOUT LIVE COVERAGE OR A JURY, THE OPENING STATEMENTS ARE KEPT BRIEF...
--AND WE INTEND TO PROVE THAT JAMES BARNES COMMITTED AN ACT OF TERROR ON AMERICAN SOIL.
--DEFENSE INTENDS TO PROVE THAT NOT ONLY IS JAMES BARNES INNOCENT...
...BUT THAT HE'S THE VICTIM OF DECADES OF MIND CONTROL AND MANIPULATION.

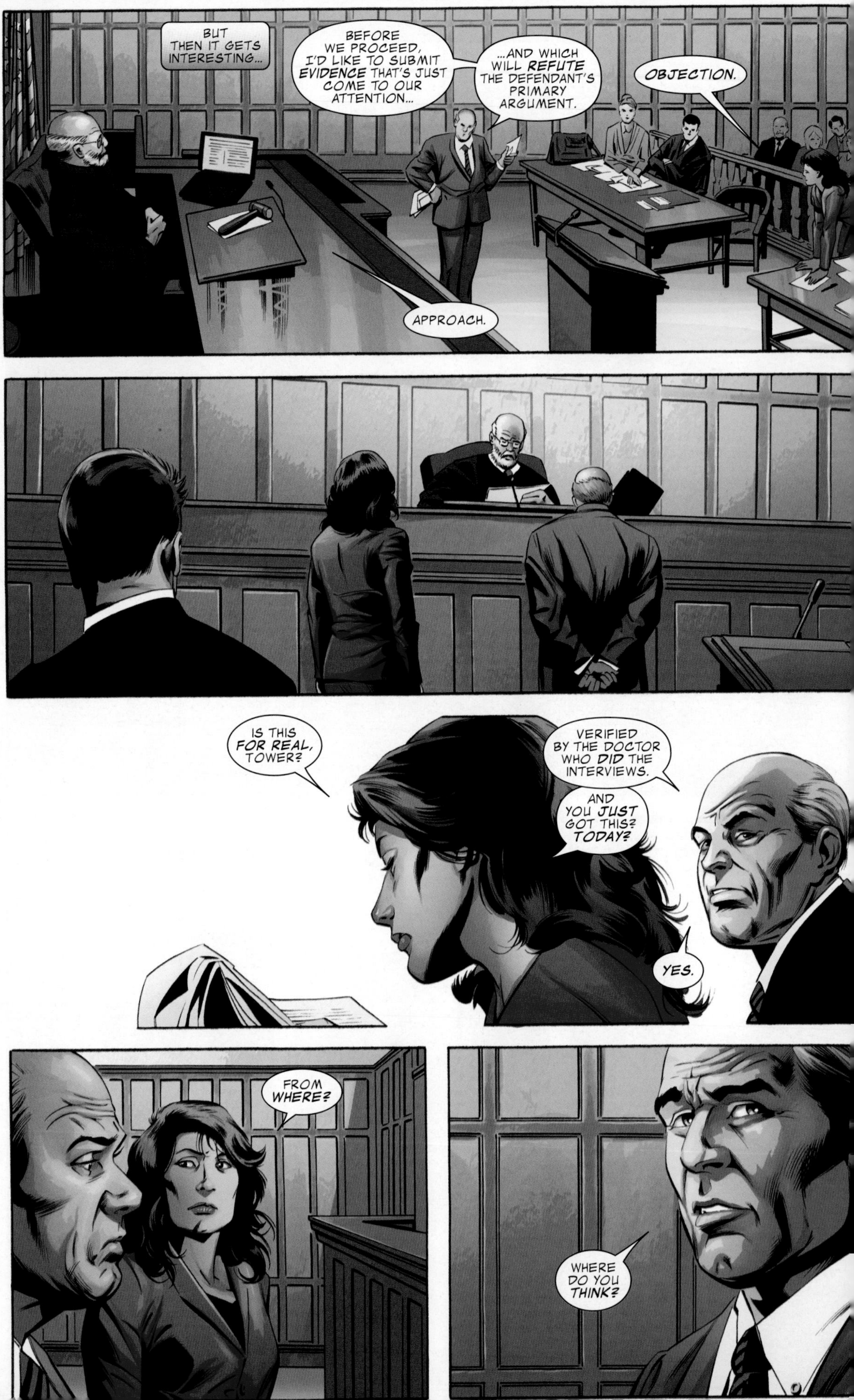
BUT THEN IT GETS INTERESTING...
BEFORE WE PROCEED, I'D LIKE TO SUBMIT EVIDENCE THAT'S JUST COME TO OUR ATTENTION...
...AND WHICH WILL REFUTE THE DEFENDANT'S PRIMARY ARGUMENT.
OBJECTION.
APPROACH.
IS THIS FOR REAL, TOWER?
VERIFIED BY THE DOCTOR WHO DID THE INTERVIEWS.
AND YOU JUST GOT THIS? TODAY?
YES.
FROM WHERE?
WHERE DO YOU THINK?

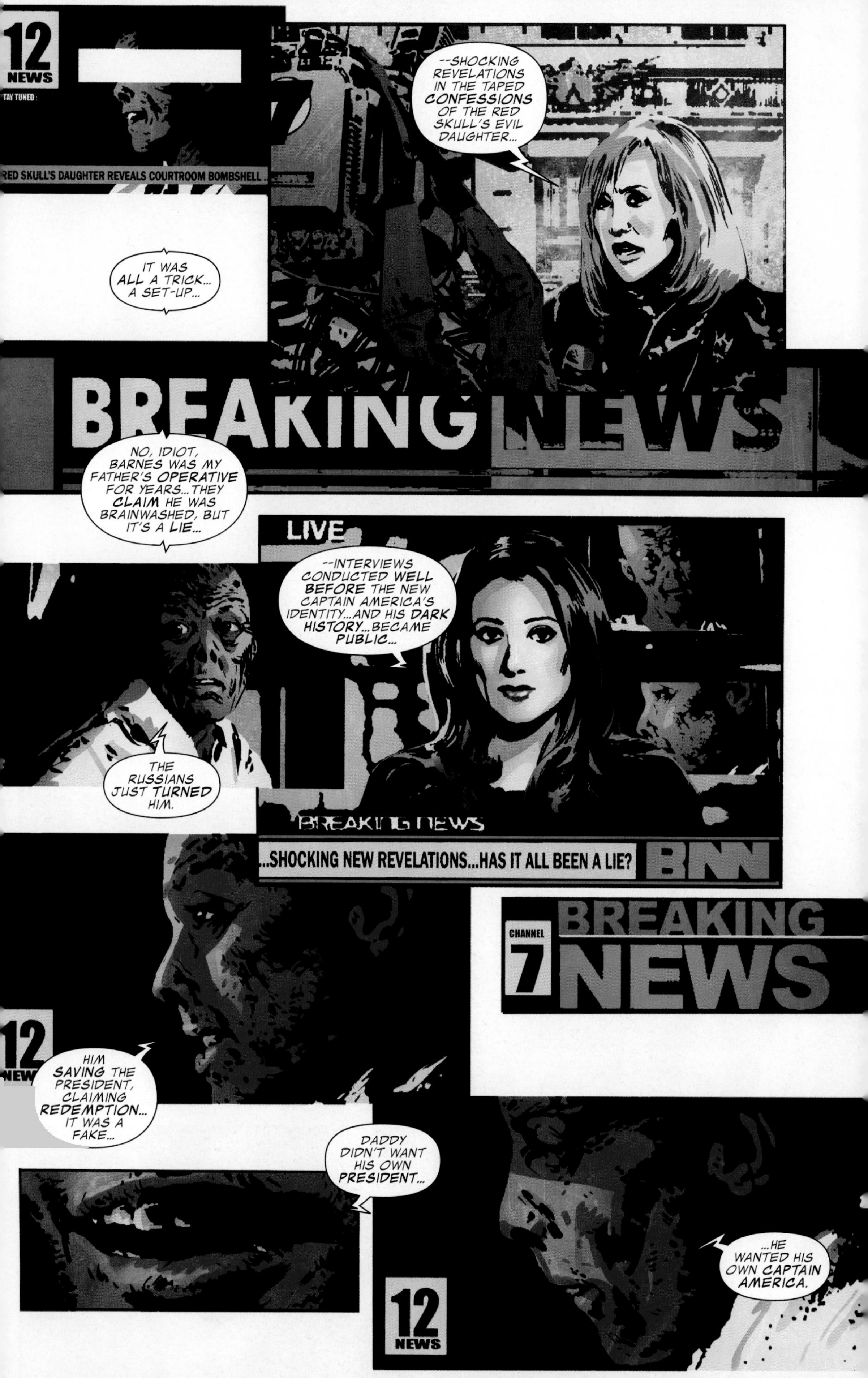
12 NEWS
TAY TUNED :
RED SKULL'S DAUGHTER REVEALS COURTROOM BOMBSHELL ...
--SHOCKING REVELATIONS IN THE TAPED CONFESSIONS OF THE RED SKULL'S EVIL DAUGHTER...
IT WAS ALL A TRICK... A SET-UP...
BREAKING NEWS
NO, IDIOT, BARNES WAS MY FATHER'S OPERATIVE FOR YEARS...THEY CLAIM HE WAS BRAINWASHED, BUT IT'S A LIE...
LIVE
--INTERVIEWS CONDUCTED WELL BEFORE THE NEW CAPTAIN AMERICA'S IDENTITY...AND HIS DARK HISTORY...BECAME PUBLIC...
THE RUSSIANS JUST TURNED HIM.
BREAKING NEWS
...SHOCKING NEW REVELATIONS...HAS IT ALL BEEN A LIE?
BNN
CHANNEL 7 BREAKING NEWS
12 NEWS
HIM SAVING THE PRESIDENT, CLAIMING REDEMPTION... IT WAS A FAKE...
DADDY DIDN'T WANT HIS OWN PRESIDENT...
...HE WANTED HIS OWN CAPTAIN AMERICA.
12 NEWS

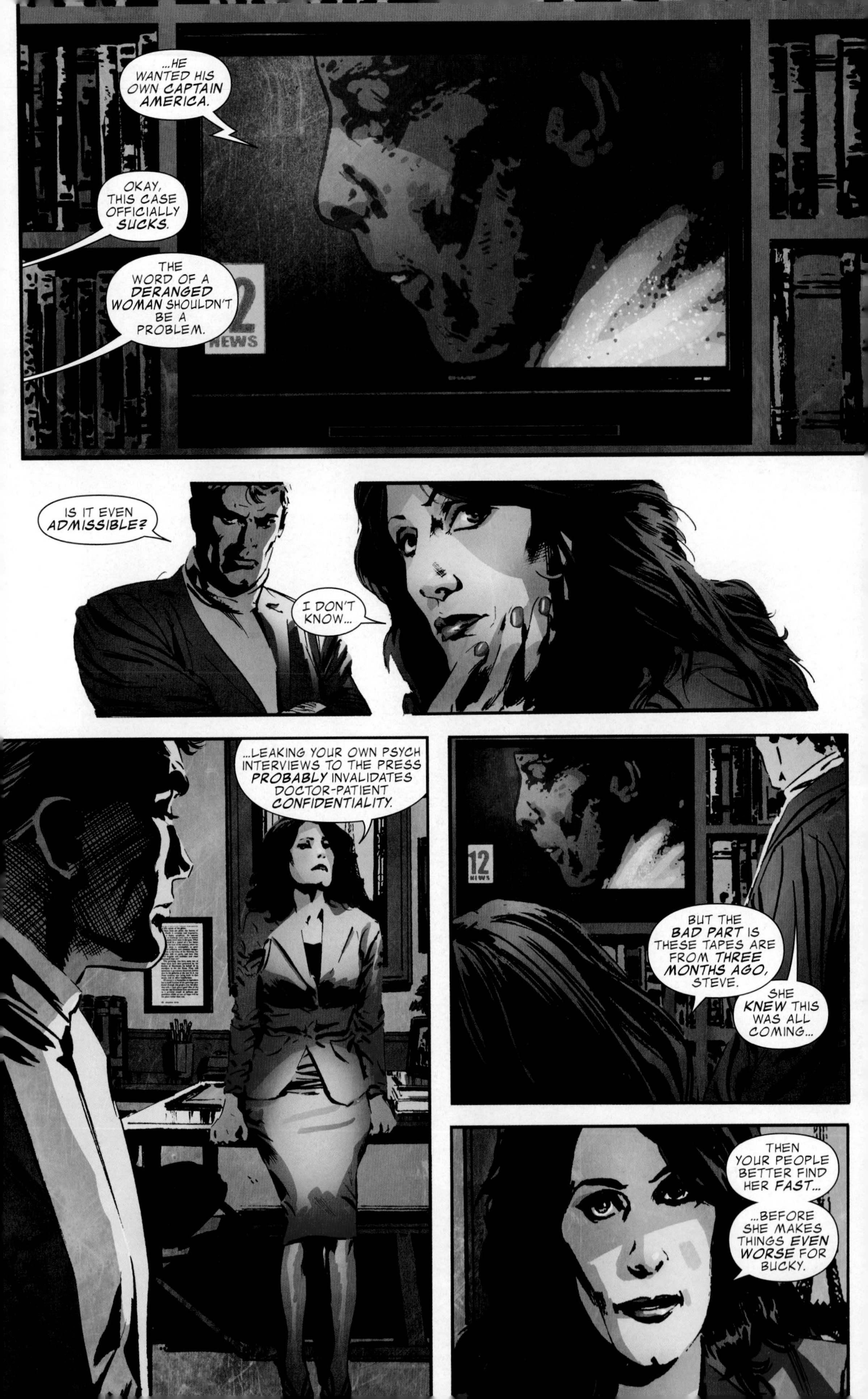
...HE WANTED HIS OWN CAPTAIN AMERICA.
OKAY, THIS CASE OFFICIALLY SUCKS.
THE WORD OF A DERANGED WOMAN SHOULDN'T BE A PROBLEM.
IS IT EVEN ADMISSIBLE?
I DON'T KNOW...
...LEAKING YOUR OWN PSYCH INTERVIEWS TO THE PRESS PROBABLY INVALIDATES DOCTOR-PATIENT CONFIDENTIALITY.
BUT THE BAD PART IS THESE TAPES ARE FROM THREE MONTHS AGO, STEVE.
SHE KNEW THIS WAS ALL COMING...
THEN YOUR PEOPLE BETTER FIND HER FAST...
...BEFORE SHE MAKES THINGS EVEN WORSE FOR BUCKY.

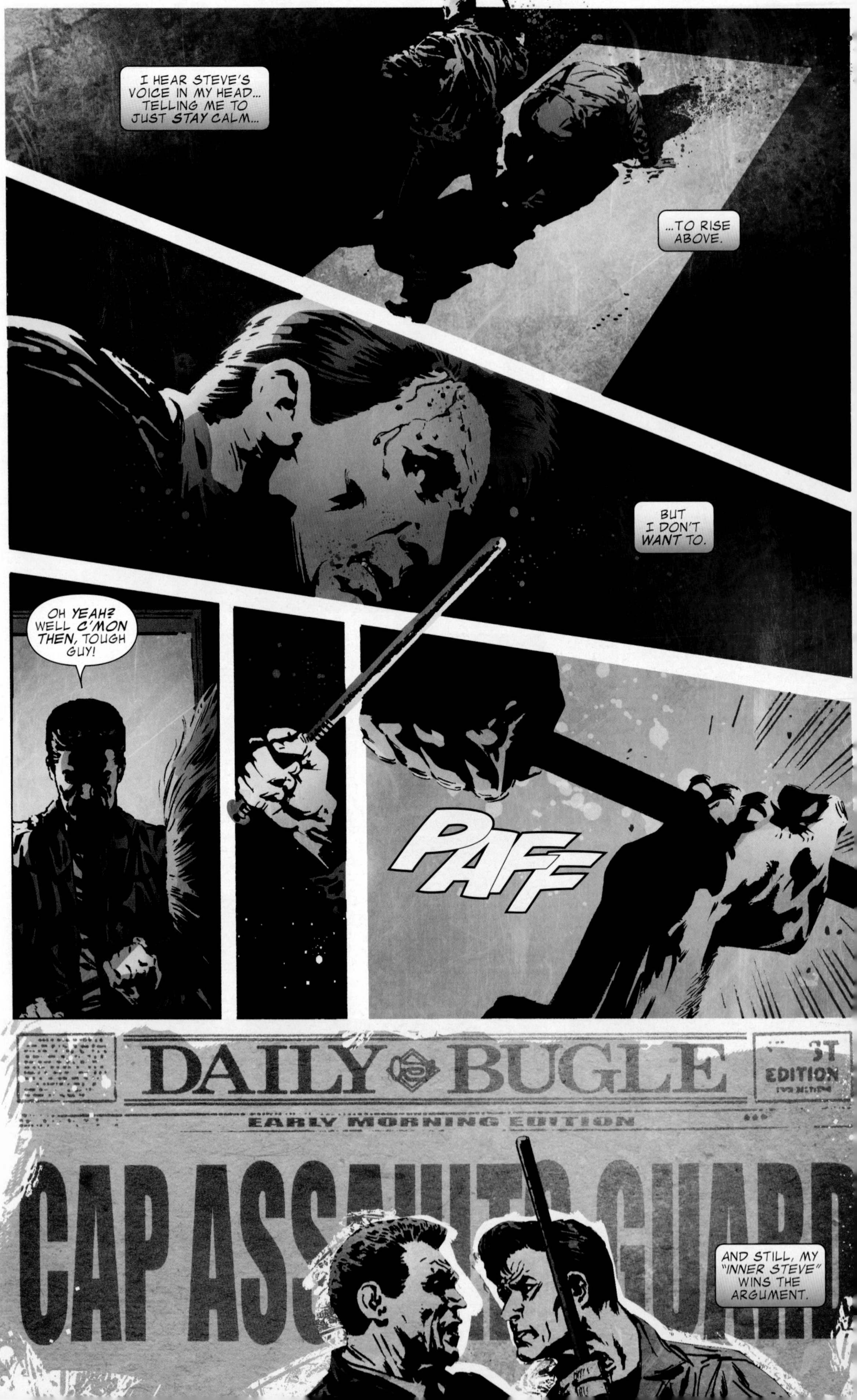
I HEAR STEVE'S VOICE IN MY HEAD... TELLING ME TO JUST STAY CALM...
...TO RISE ABOVE.
BUT I DON'T WANT TO.
OH YEAH? WELL C'MON THEN, TOUGH GUY!
PAFF
DAILY BUGLE
EARLY MORNING EDITION
CAP ASSAULTS GUARD
AND STILL, MY "INNER STEVE" WINS THE ARGUMENT.

'CAUSE HE'S RIGHT...

LET'S JUST LEAVE IT...OKAY?

...THE *LAST THING* WE NEED IS *ME* FEEDING THE PRESS FROM IN HERE.

SO I SWALLOW WHAT'S *LEFT* OF MY PRIDE...

...AND REMEMBER THIS IS ABOUT *REDEMPTION*...NOT ANYTHING ELSE.

PSSSH... KNEW YOU DIDN'T HAVE ANY *GUTS*...

HOLDING BLOCK

AND IT'S NOT *SUPPOSED* TO BE EASY.

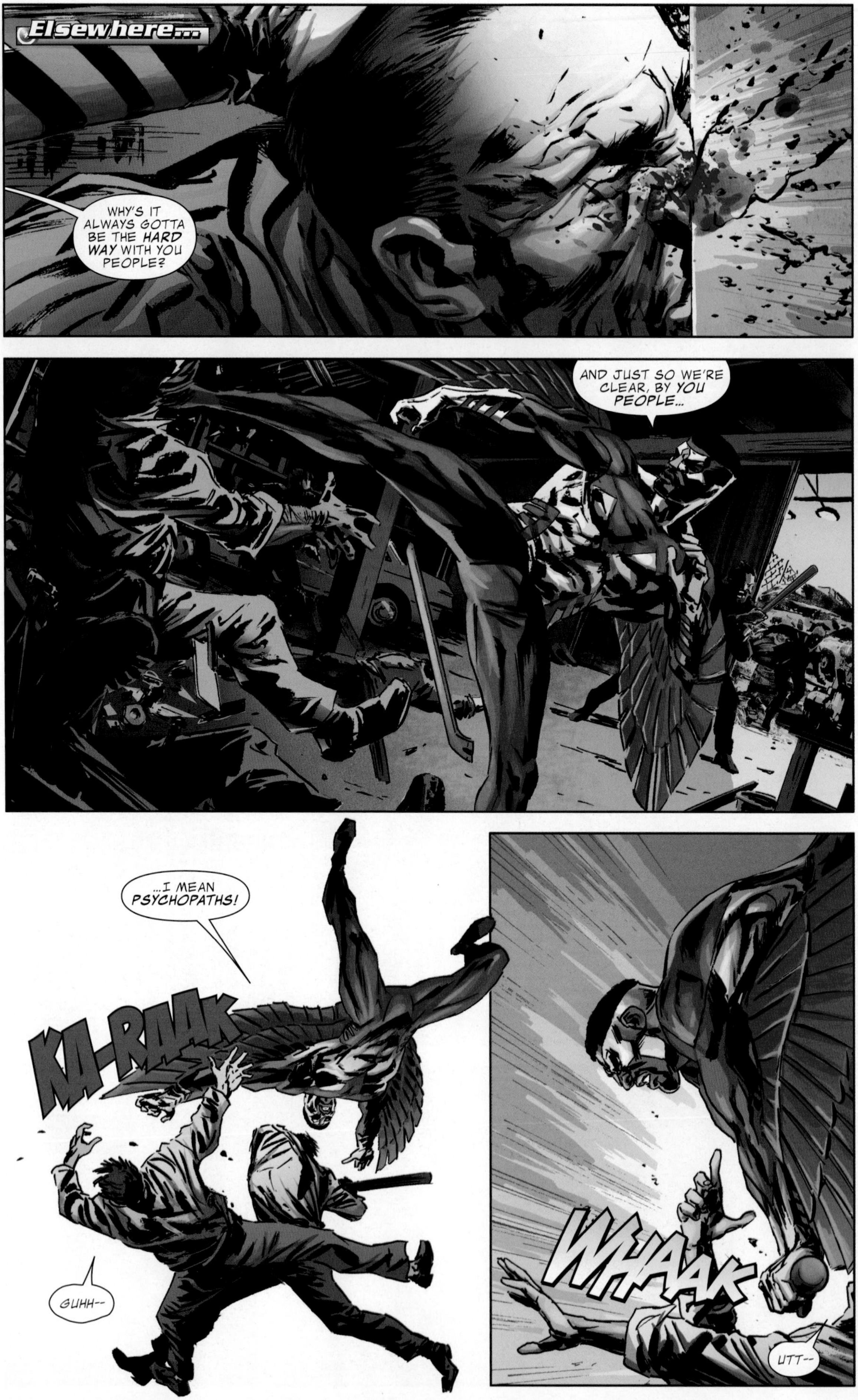
Elsewhere...
WHY'S IT ALWAYS GOTTA BE THE HARD WAY WITH YOU PEOPLE?
AND JUST SO WE'RE CLEAR, BY YOU PEOPLE...
...I MEAN PSYCHOPATHS!
KA-RAAK
GUHH--
WHAAK
UTT--

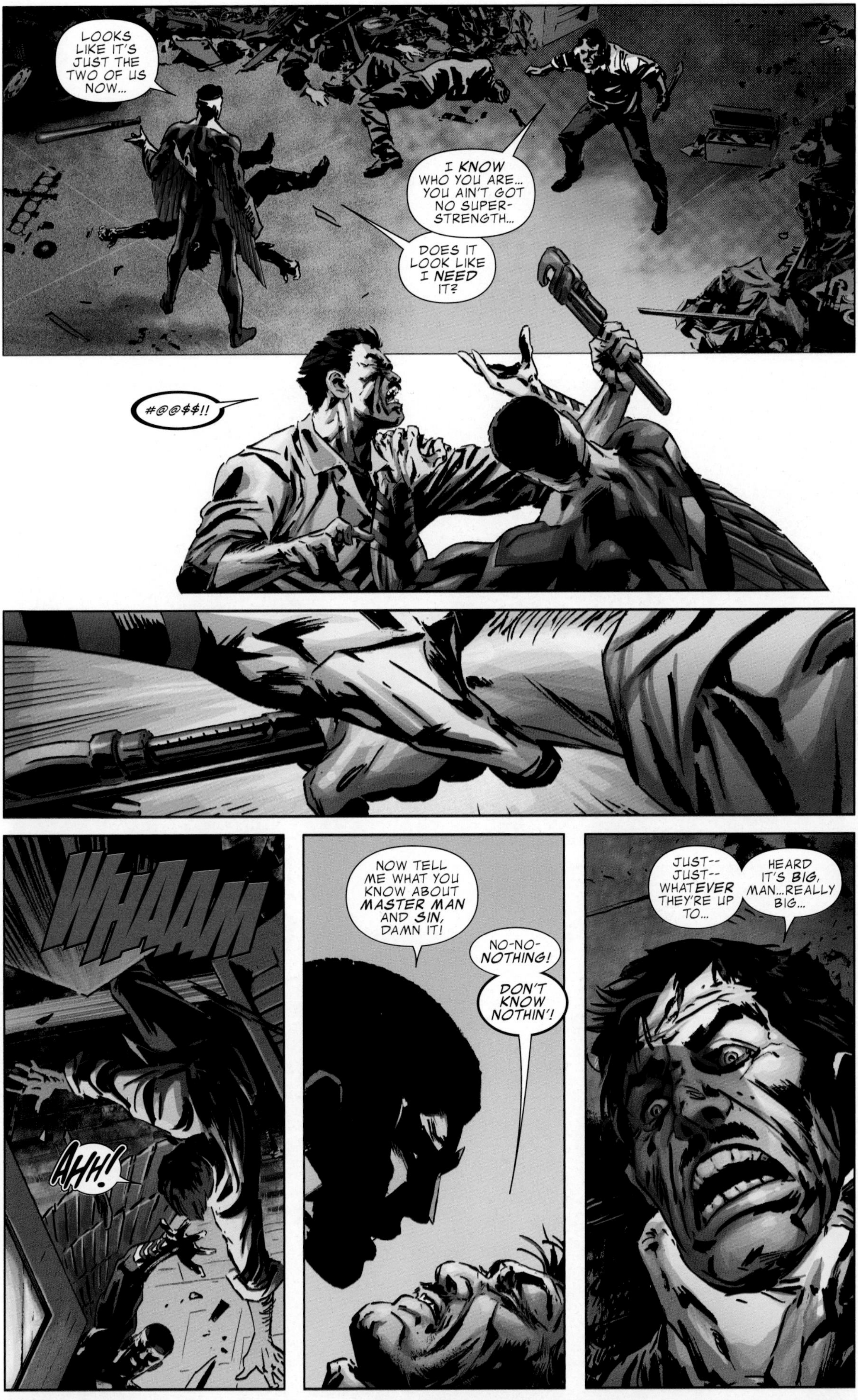
LOOKS LIKE IT'S JUST THE TWO OF US NOW...
I KNOW WHO YOU ARE... YOU AIN'T GOT NO SUPER-STRENGTH...
DOES IT LOOK LIKE I NEED IT?
#@@$$!!
WHAAM
AHH!
NOW TELL ME WHAT YOU KNOW ABOUT MASTER MAN AND SIN, DAMN IT!
NO-NO-NOTHING!
DON'T KNOW NOTHIN'!
JUST--JUST--WHATEVER THEY'RE UP TO...
HEARD IT'S BIG, MAN...REALLY BIG...

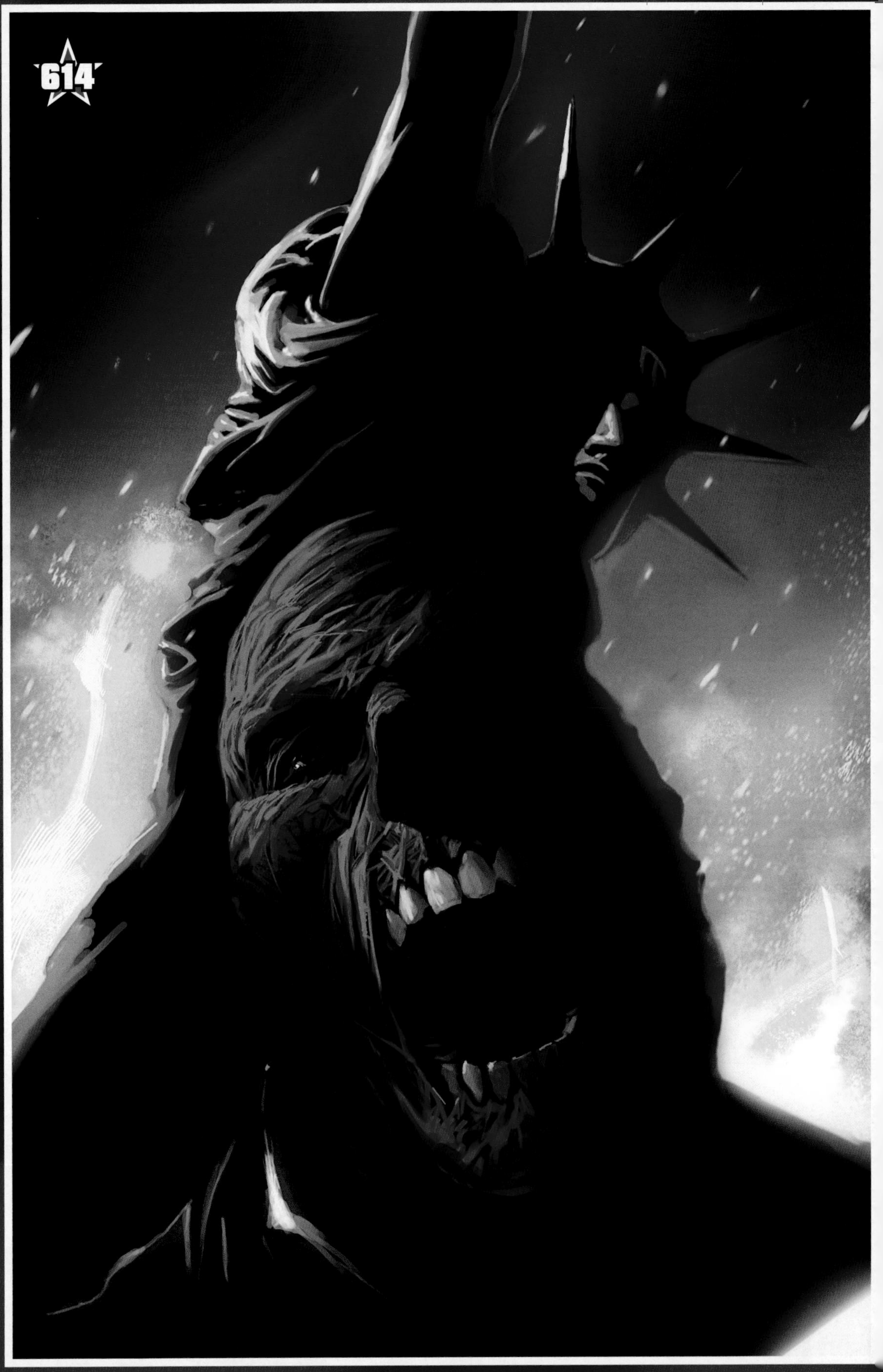
614

THE TRIAL OF CAPTAIN AMERICA PART 4

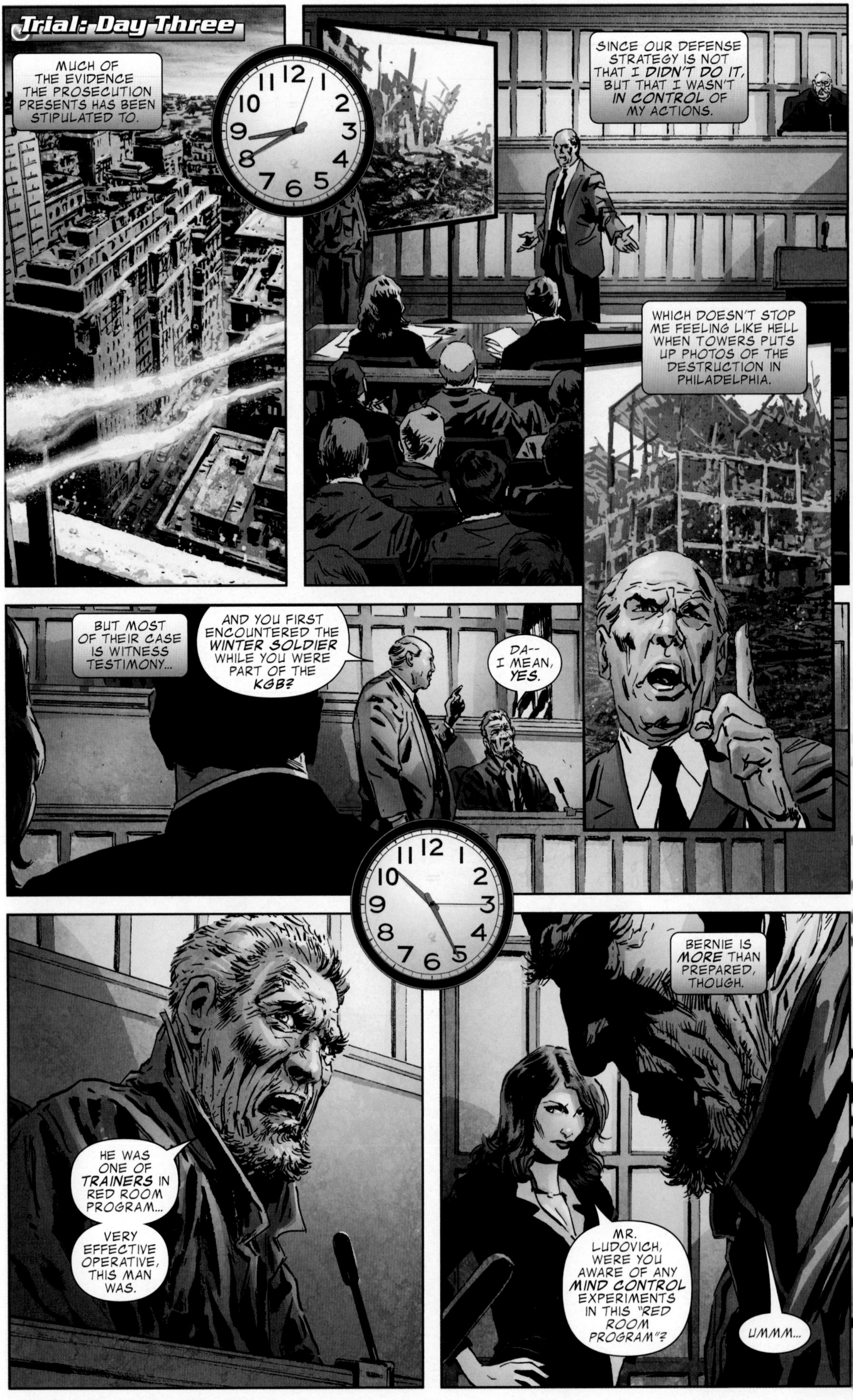
Trial: Day Three
MUCH OF THE EVIDENCE THE PROSECUTION PRESENTS HAS BEEN STIPULATED TO.
SINCE OUR DEFENSE STRATEGY IS NOT THAT I DIDN'T DO IT, BUT THAT I WASN'T IN CONTROL OF MY ACTIONS.
WHICH DOESN'T STOP ME FEELING LIKE HELL WHEN TOWERS PUTS UP PHOTOS OF THE DESTRUCTION IN PHILADELPHIA.
BUT MOST OF THEIR CASE IS WITNESS TESTIMONY...
AND YOU FIRST ENCOUNTERED THE WINTER SOLDIER WHILE YOU WERE PART OF THE KGB?
DA-- I MEAN, YES.
BERNIE IS MORE THAN PREPARED, THOUGH.
HE WAS ONE OF TRAINERS IN RED ROOM PROGRAM...
VERY EFFECTIVE OPERATIVE, THIS MAN WAS.
MR. LUDOVICH, WERE YOU AWARE OF ANY MIND CONTROL EXPERIMENTS IN THIS "RED ROOM PROGRAM"?
UMMM...

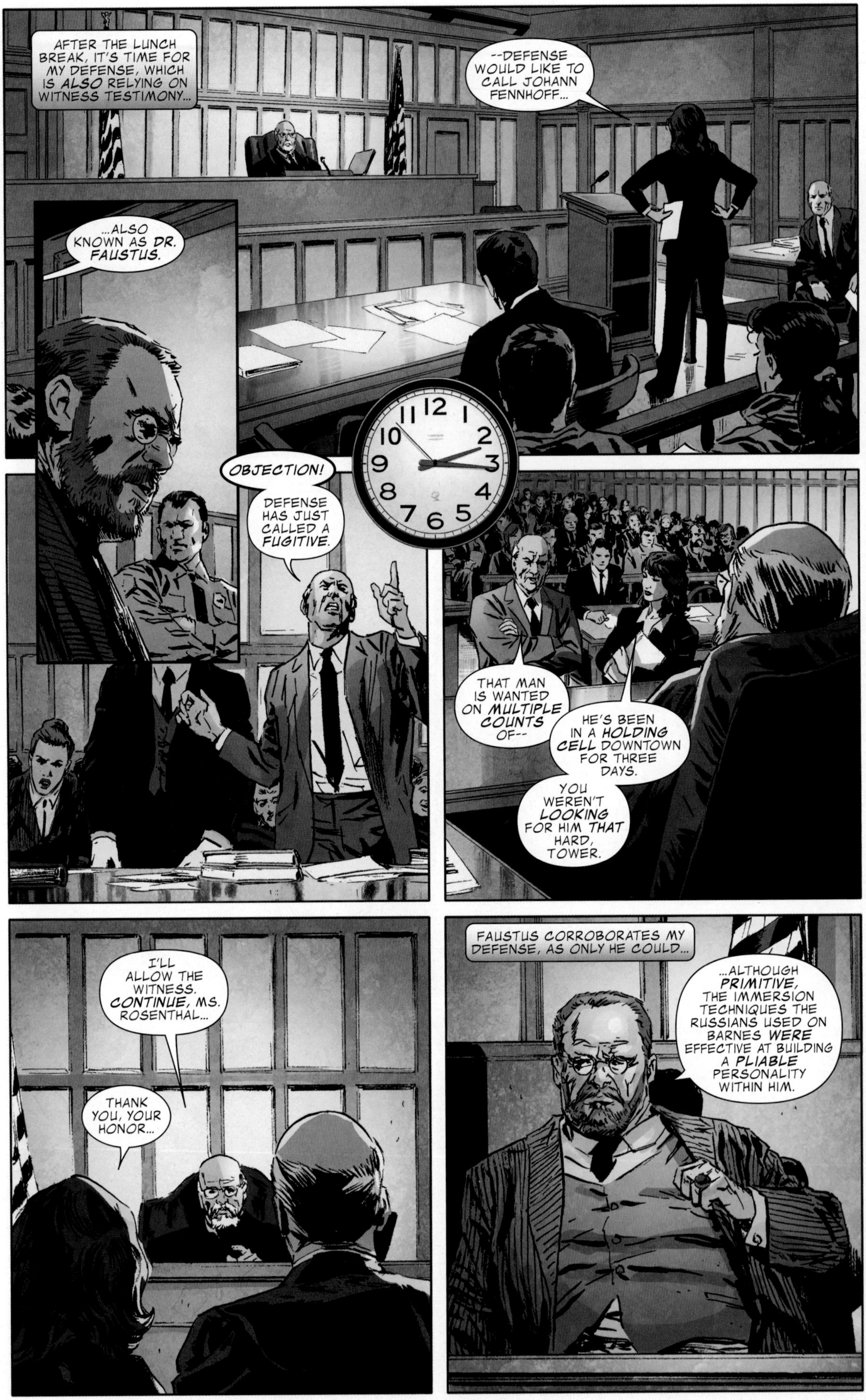

AFTER THE LUNCH BREAK, IT'S TIME FOR MY DEFENSE, WHICH IS ALSO RELYING ON WITNESS TESTIMONY...
--DEFENSE WOULD LIKE TO CALL JOHANN FENNHOFF...
...ALSO KNOWN AS DR. FAUSTUS.
12
1
2
3
4
5
6
7
8
9
10
11
OBJECTION!
DEFENSE HAS JUST CALLED A FUGITIVE.
THAT MAN IS WANTED ON MULTIPLE COUNTS OF--
HE'S BEEN IN A HOLDING CELL DOWNTOWN FOR THREE DAYS.
YOU WEREN'T LOOKING FOR HIM THAT HARD, TOWER.
I'LL ALLOW THE WITNESS. CONTINUE, MS. ROSENTHAL...
THANK YOU, YOUR HONOR...
FAUSTUS CORROBORATES MY DEFENSE, AS ONLY HE COULD...
...ALTHOUGH PRIMITIVE, THE IMMERSION TECHNIQUES THE RUSSIANS USED ON BARNES WERE EFFECTIVE AT BUILDING A PLIABLE PERSONALITY WITHIN HIM.

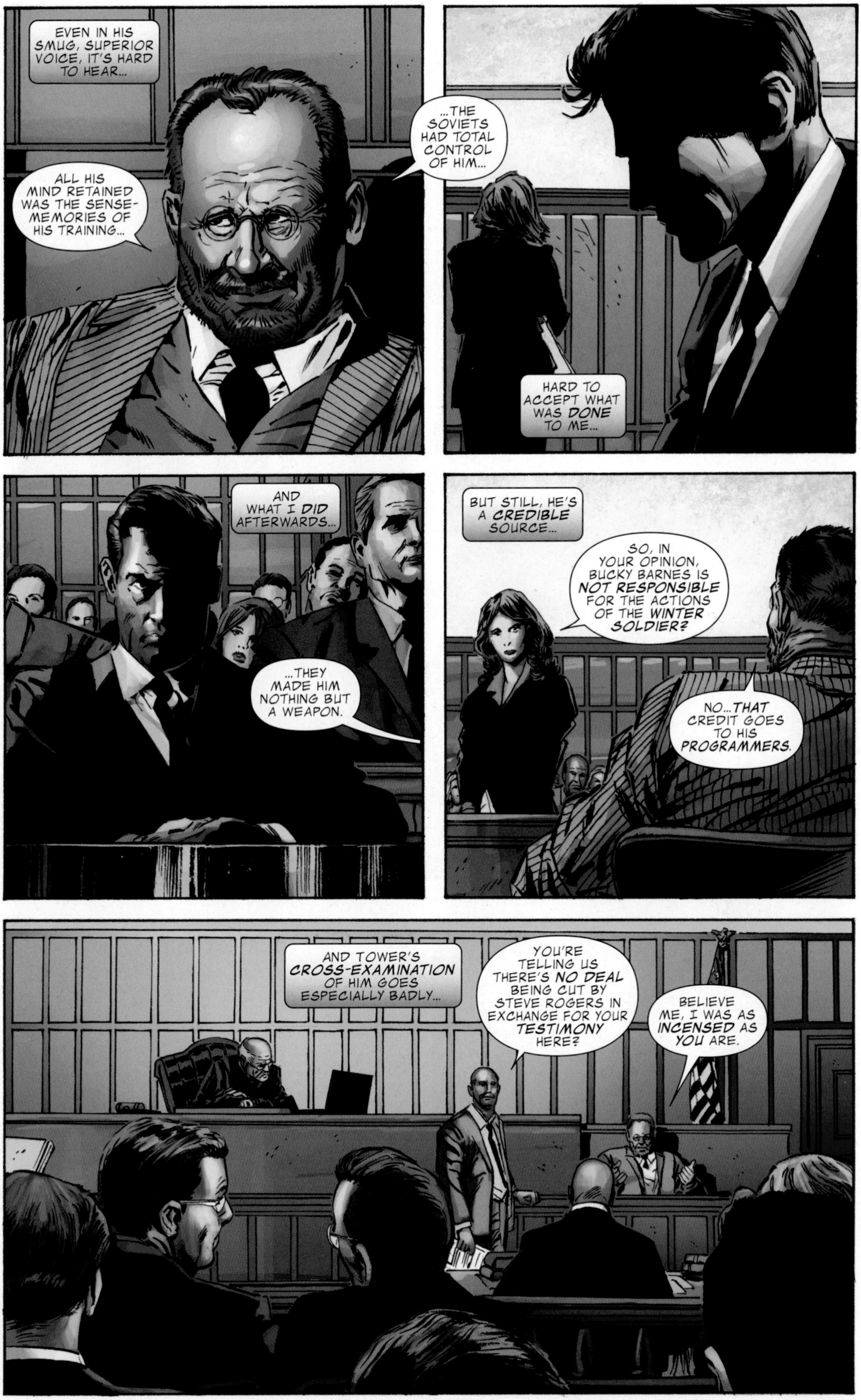
EVEN IN HIS SMUG, SUPERIOR VOICE, IT'S HARD TO HEAR...
ALL HIS MIND RETAINED WAS THE SENSE-MEMORIES OF HIS TRAINING...
...THE SOVIETS HAD TOTAL CONTROL OF HIM...
HARD TO ACCEPT WHAT WAS DONE TO ME...
AND WHAT I DID AFTERWARDS...
...THEY MADE HIM NOTHING BUT A WEAPON.
BUT STILL, HE'S A CREDIBLE SOURCE...
SO, IN YOUR OPINION, BUCKY BARNES IS NOT RESPONSIBLE FOR THE ACTIONS OF THE WINTER SOLDIER?
NO...THAT CREDIT GOES TO HIS PROGRAMMERS.
AND TOWER'S CROSS-EXAMINATION OF HIM GOES ESPECIALLY BADLY...
YOU'RE TELLING US THERE'S NO DEAL BEING CUT BY STEVE ROGERS IN EXCHANGE FOR YOUR TESTIMONY HERE?
BELIEVE ME, I WAS AS INCENSED AS YOU ARE.

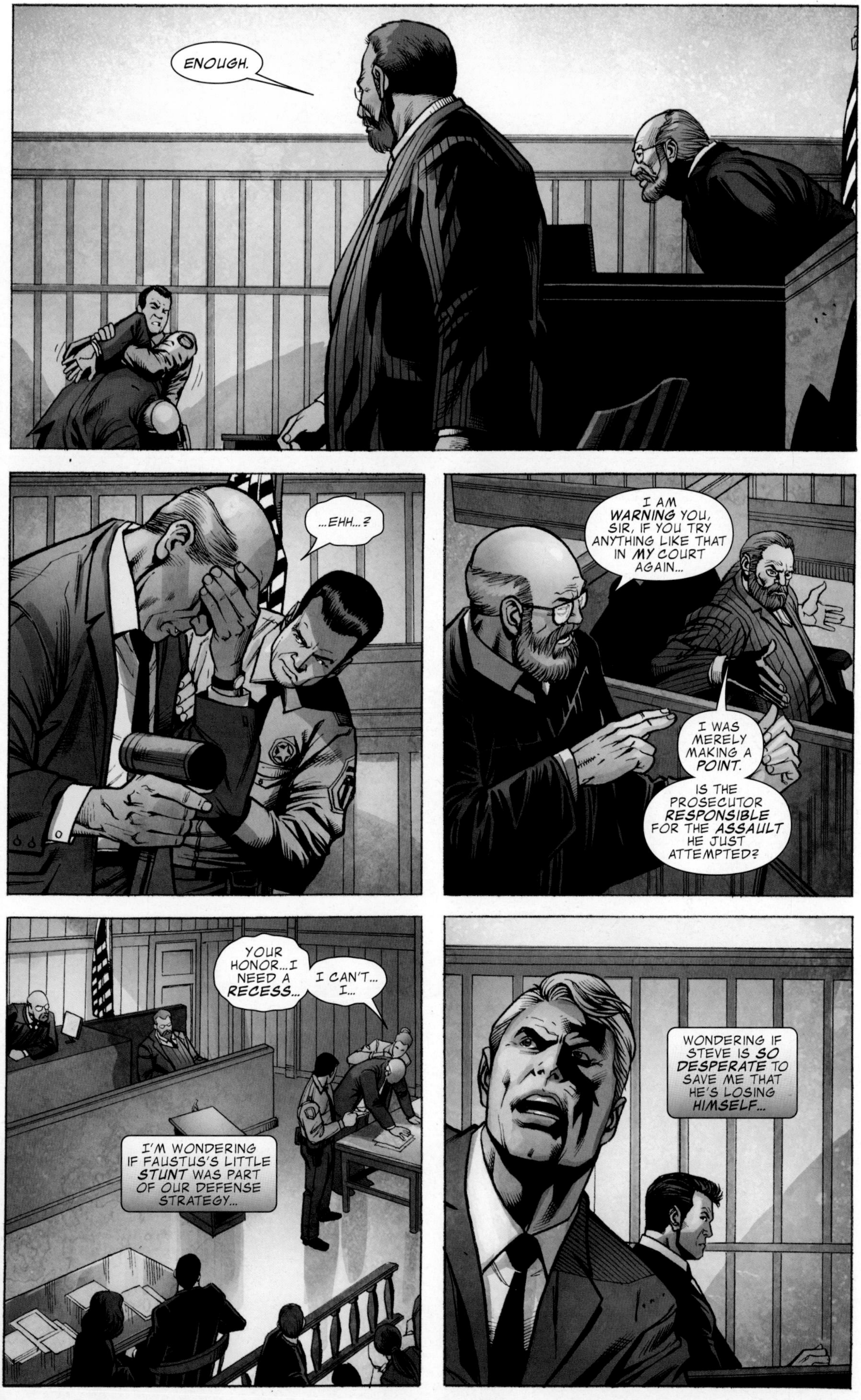

ENOUGH.
...EHH...?
I AM WARNING YOU, SIR, IF YOU TRY ANYTHING LIKE THAT IN MY COURT AGAIN...
I WAS MERELY MAKING A POINT.
IS THE PROSECUTOR RESPONSIBLE FOR THE ASSAULT HE JUST ATTEMPTED?
YOUR HONOR...I NEED A RECESS...
I CAN'T... I...
I'M WONDERING IF FAUSTUS'S LITTLE STUNT WAS PART OF OUR DEFENSE STRATEGY...
WONDERING IF STEVE IS SO DESPERATE TO SAVE ME THAT HE'S LOSING HIMSELF...

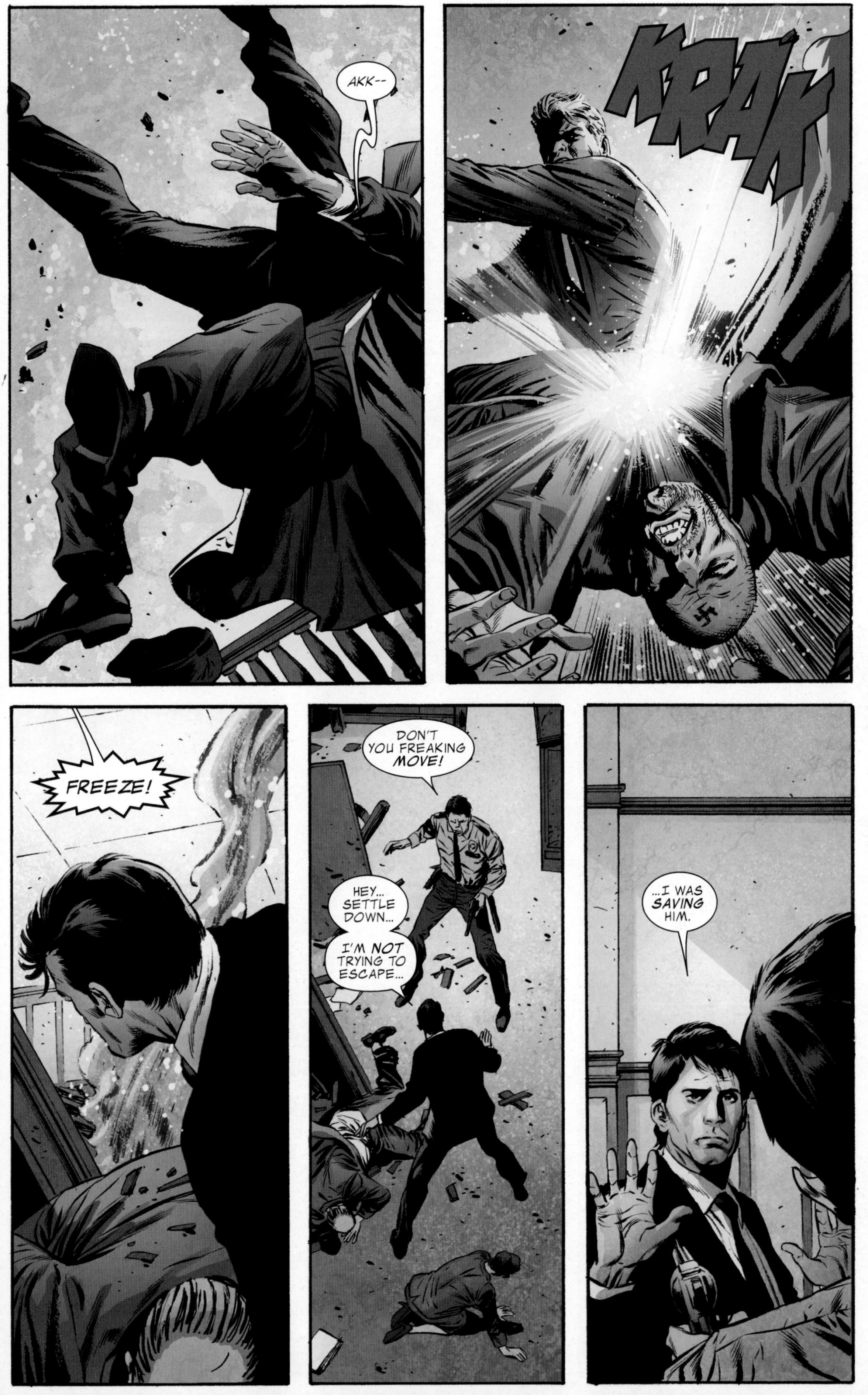

AKK--
KRAK!
FREEZE!
DON'T YOU FREAKING MOVE!
HEY... SETTLE DOWN...
I'M NOT TRYING TO ESCAPE...
...I WAS SAVING HIM.

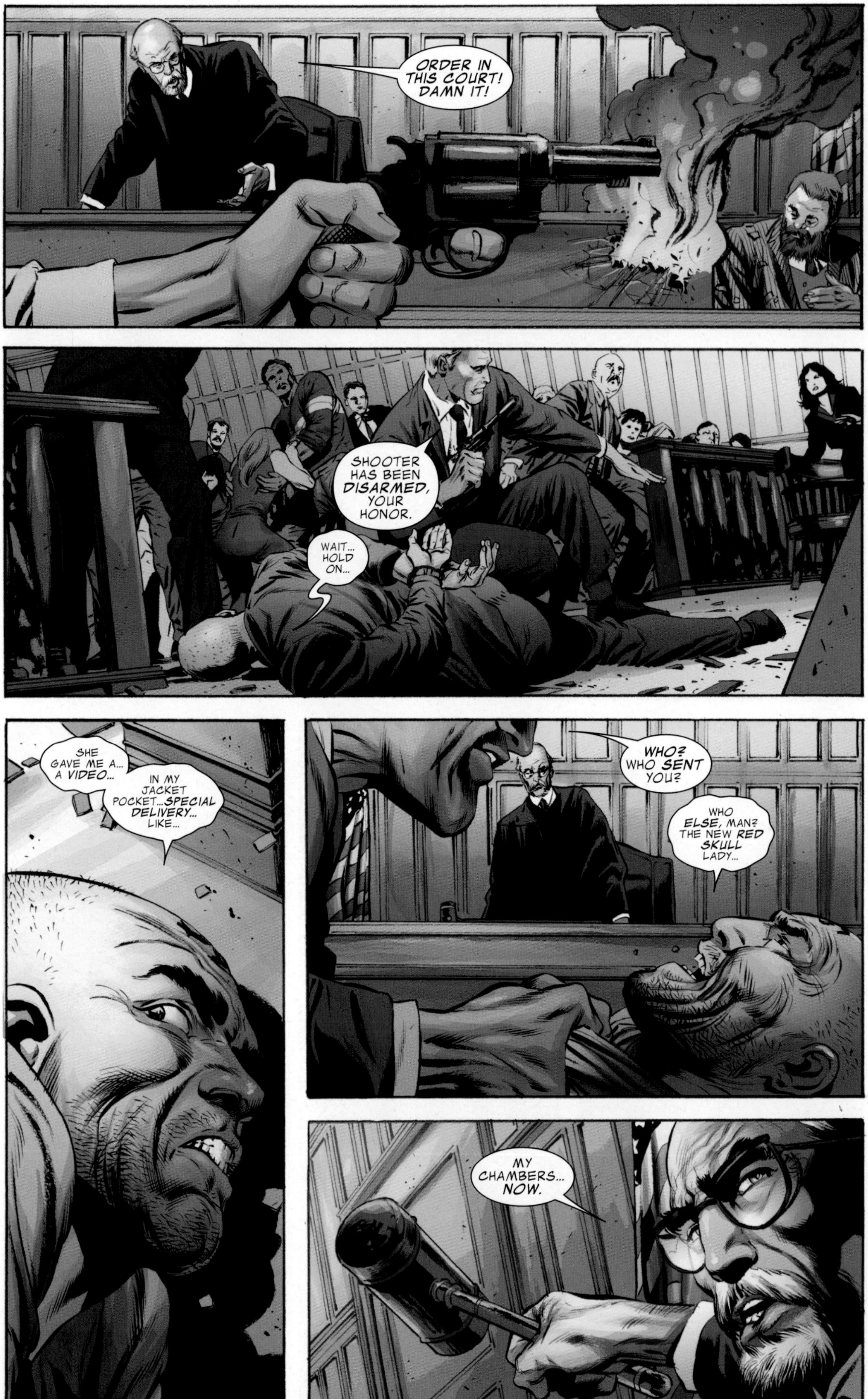
ORDER IN THIS COURT! DAMN IT!
SHOOTER HAS BEEN DISARMED, YOUR HONOR.
WAIT... HOLD ON...
SHE GAVE ME A... A VIDEO...
IN MY JACKET POCKET...SPECIAL DELIVERY... LIKE...
WHO? WHO SENT YOU?
WHO ELSE, MAN? THE NEW RED SKULL LADY...
MY CHAMBERS... NOW.

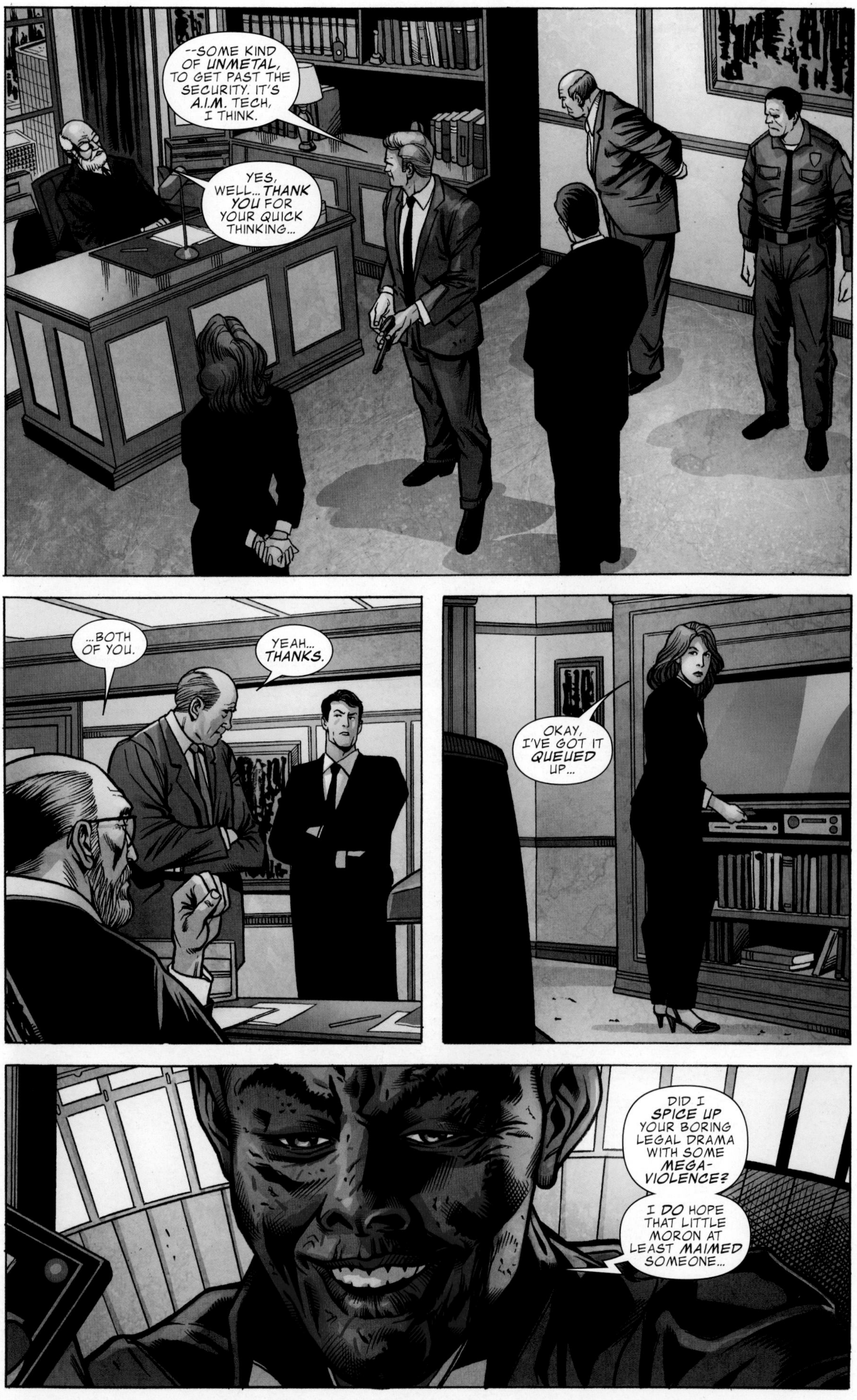
--SOME KIND OF UNMETAL, TO GET PAST THE SECURITY. IT'S A.I.M. TECH, I THINK.
YES, WELL... THANK YOU FOR YOUR QUICK THINKING...
...BOTH OF YOU.
YEAH... THANKS.
OKAY, I'VE GOT IT QUEUED UP...
DID I SPICE UP YOUR BORING LEGAL DRAMA WITH SOME MEGA-VIOLENCE?
I DO HOPE THAT LITTLE MORON AT LEAST MAIMED SOMEONE...

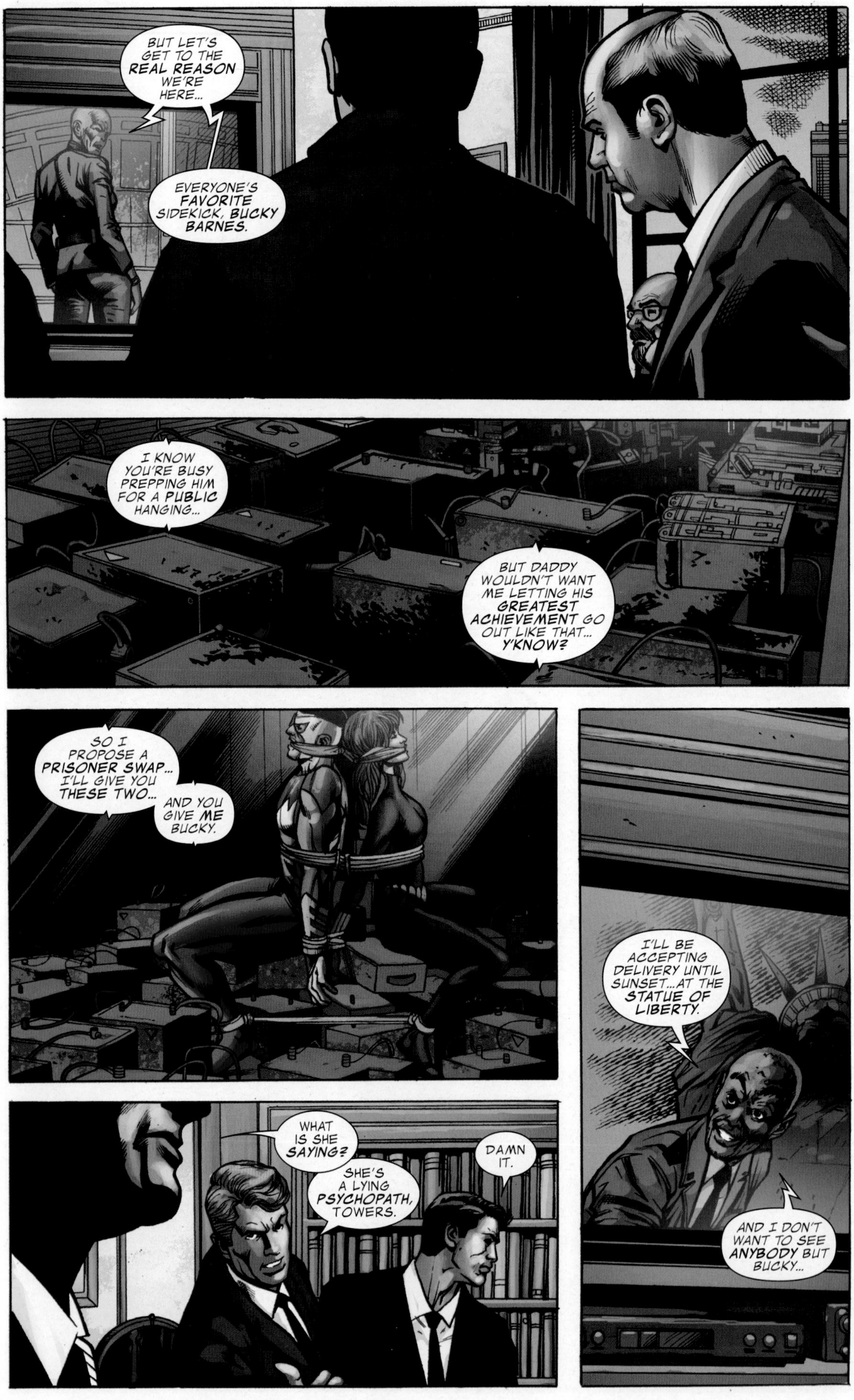
BUT LET'S GET TO THE REAL REASON WE'RE HERE...
EVERYONE'S FAVORITE SIDEKICK, BUCKY BARNES.
I KNOW YOU'RE BUSY PREPPING HIM FOR A PUBLIC HANGING...
BUT DADDY WOULDN'T WANT ME LETTING HIS GREATEST ACHIEVEMENT GO OUT LIKE THAT... Y'KNOW?
SO I PROPOSE A PRISONER SWAP... I'LL GIVE YOU THESE TWO...
AND YOU GIVE ME BUCKY.
I'LL BE ACCEPTING DELIVERY UNTIL SUNSET...AT THE STATUE OF LIBERTY.
AND I DON'T WANT TO SEE ANYBODY BUT BUCKY...
WHAT IS SHE SAYING?
SHE'S A LYING PSYCHOPATH, TOWERS.
DAMN IT.

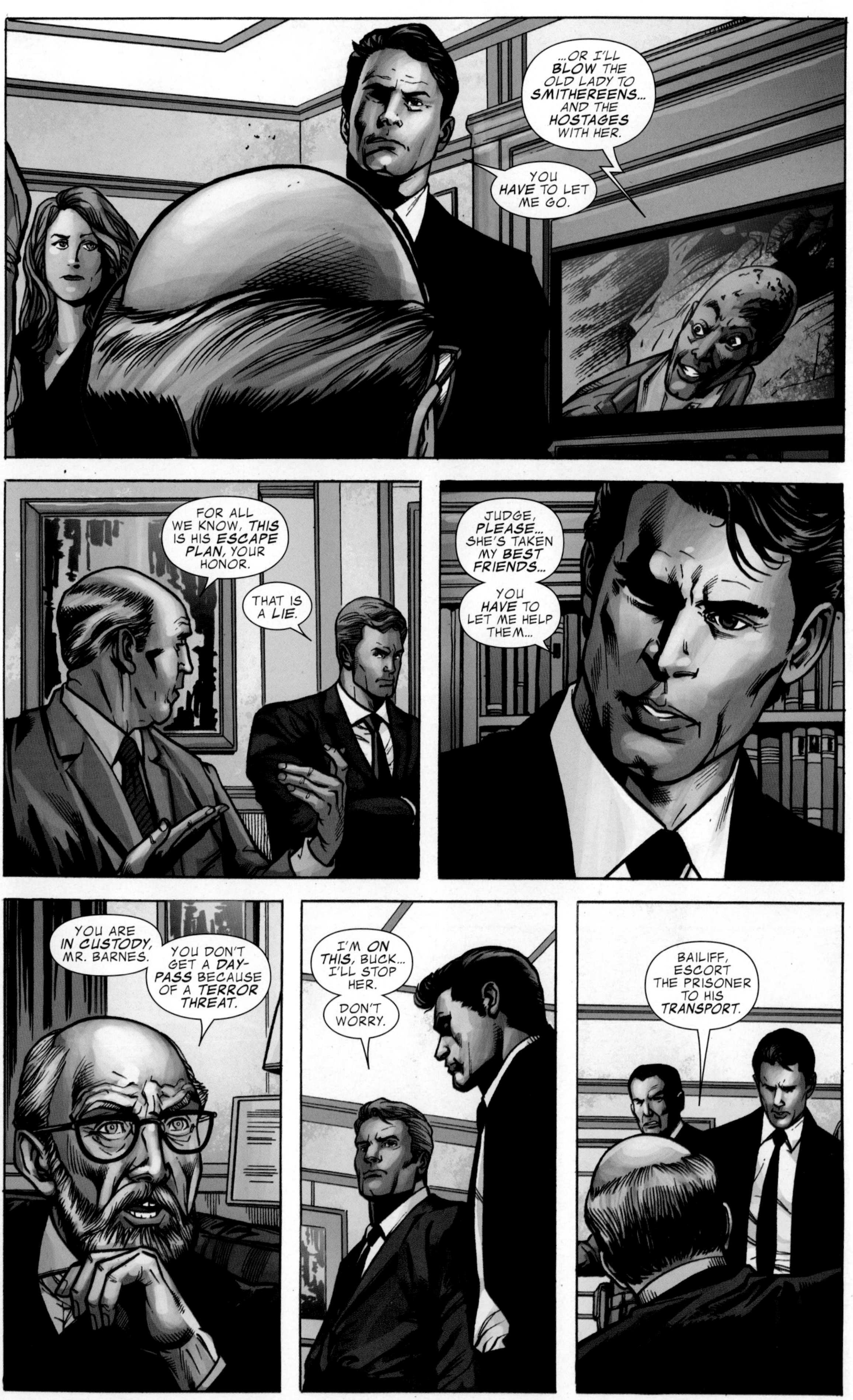
...OR I'LL BLOW THE OLD LADY TO SMITHEREENS... AND THE HOSTAGES WITH HER.
YOU HAVE TO LET ME GO.
FOR ALL WE KNOW, THIS IS HIS ESCAPE PLAN, YOUR HONOR.
THAT IS A LIE.
JUDGE, PLEASE... SHE'S TAKEN MY BEST FRIENDS...
YOU HAVE TO LET ME HELP THEM...
YOU ARE IN CUSTODY, MR. BARNES.
YOU DON'T GET A DAY-PASS BECAUSE OF A TERROR THREAT.
I'M ON THIS, BUCK... I'LL STOP HER.
DON'T WORRY.
BAILIFF, ESCORT THE PRISONER TO HIS TRANSPORT.

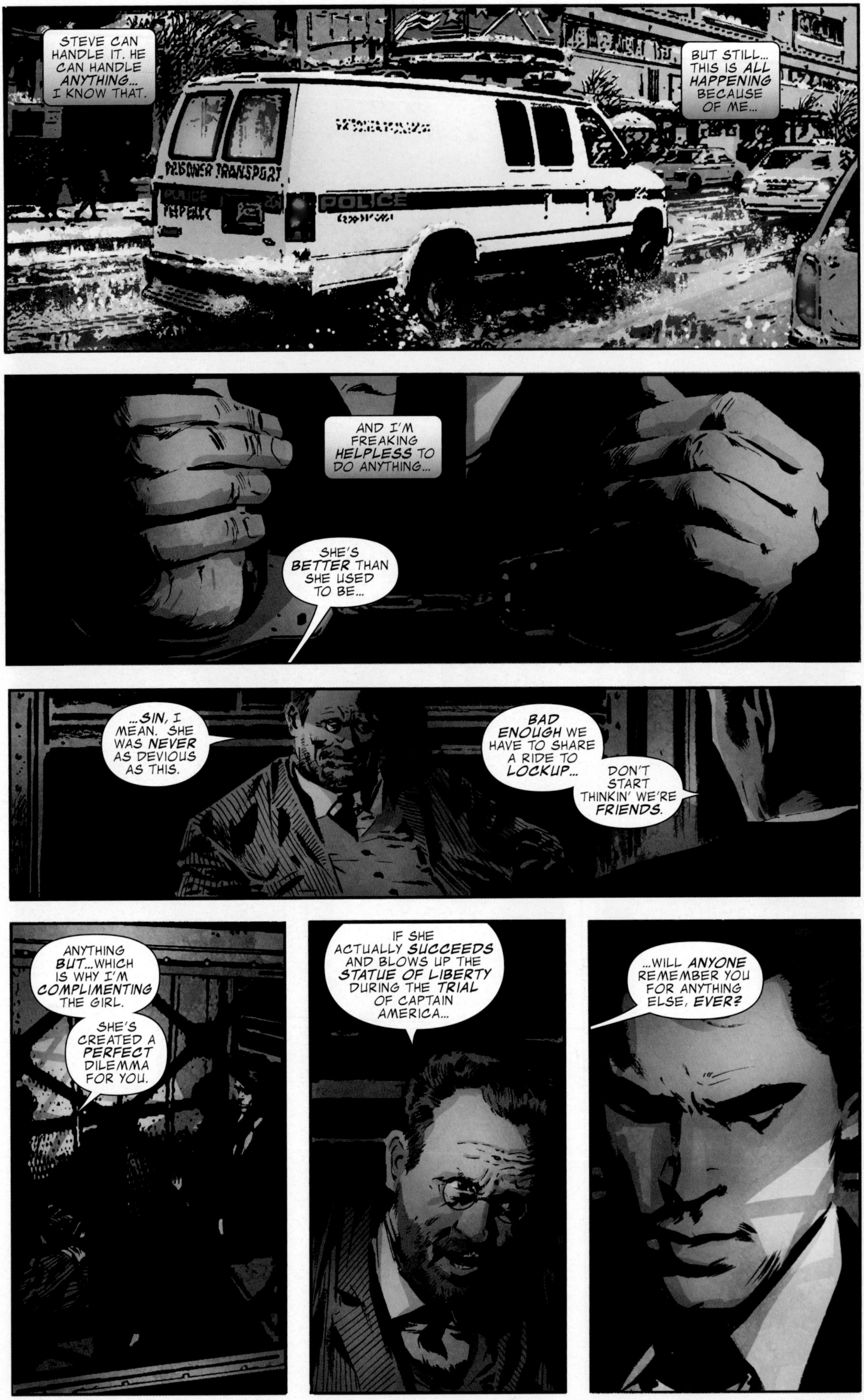
STEVE CAN HANDLE IT. HE CAN HANDLE ANYTHING... I KNOW THAT.
BUT STILL... THIS IS ALL HAPPENING BECAUSE OF ME...
PRISONER TRANSPORT
POLICE
AND I'M FREAKING HELPLESS TO DO ANYTHING...
SHE'S BETTER THAN SHE USED TO BE...
...SIN, I MEAN. SHE WAS NEVER AS DEVIOUS AS THIS.
BAD ENOUGH WE HAVE TO SHARE A RIDE TO LOCKUP...
DON'T START THINKIN' WE'RE FRIENDS.
ANYTHING BUT...WHICH IS WHY I'M COMPLIMENTING THE GIRL.
SHE'S CREATED A PERFECT DILEMMA FOR YOU.
IF SHE ACTUALLY SUCCEEDS AND BLOWS UP THE STATUE OF LIBERTY DURING THE TRIAL OF CAPTAIN AMERICA...
...WILL ANYONE REMEMBER YOU FOR ANYTHING ELSE, EVER?

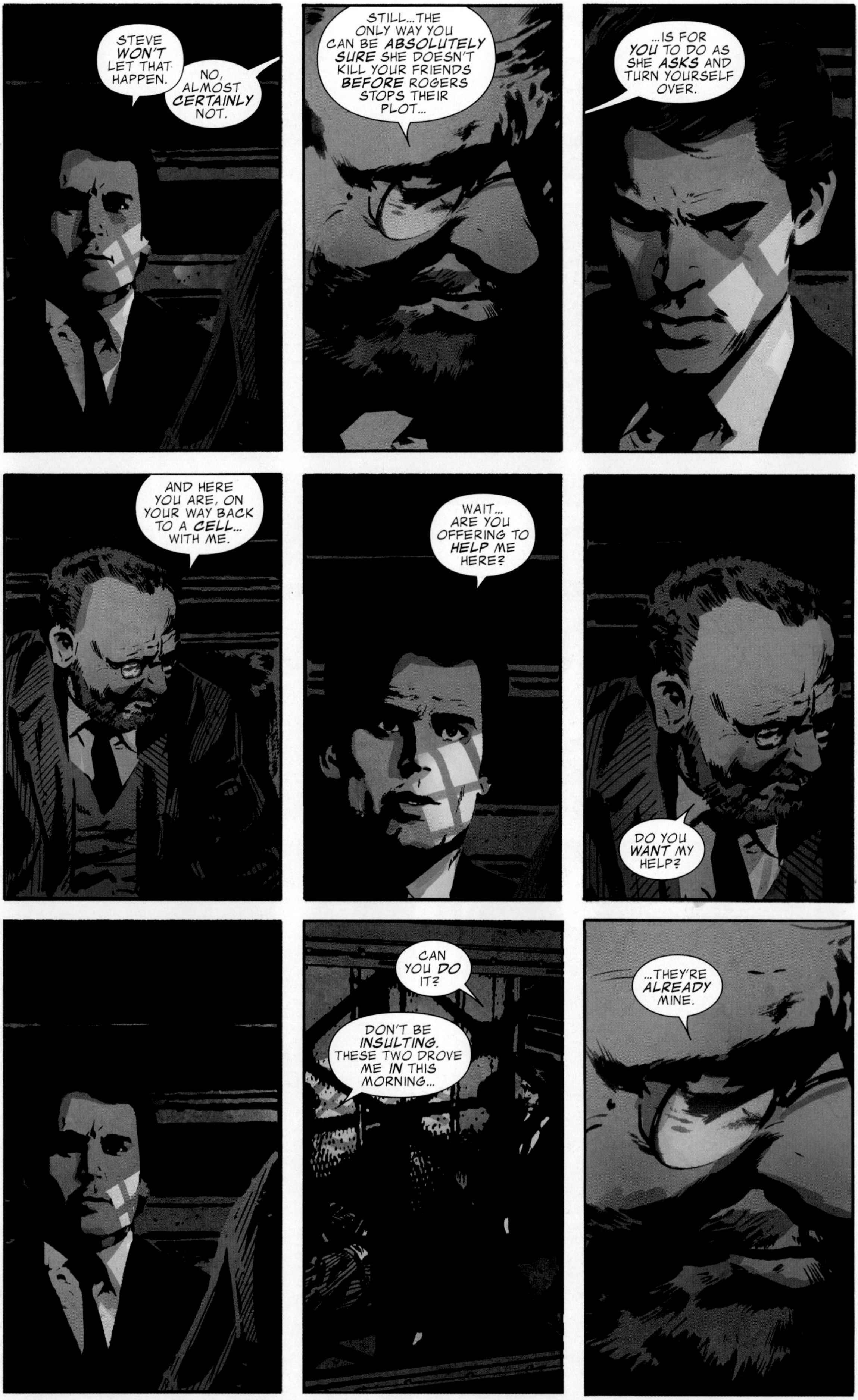
STEVE WON'T LET THAT HAPPEN.
NO, ALMOST CERTAINLY NOT.
STILL...THE ONLY WAY YOU CAN BE ABSOLUTELY SURE SHE DOESN'T KILL YOUR FRIENDS BEFORE ROGERS STOPS THEIR PLOT...
...IS FOR YOU TO DO AS SHE ASKS AND TURN YOURSELF OVER.
AND HERE YOU ARE, ON YOUR WAY BACK TO A CELL... WITH ME.
WAIT... ARE YOU OFFERING TO HELP ME HERE?
DO YOU WANT MY HELP?
CAN YOU DO IT?
DON'T BE INSULTING. THESE TWO DROVE ME IN THIS MORNING...
...THEY'RE ALREADY MINE.

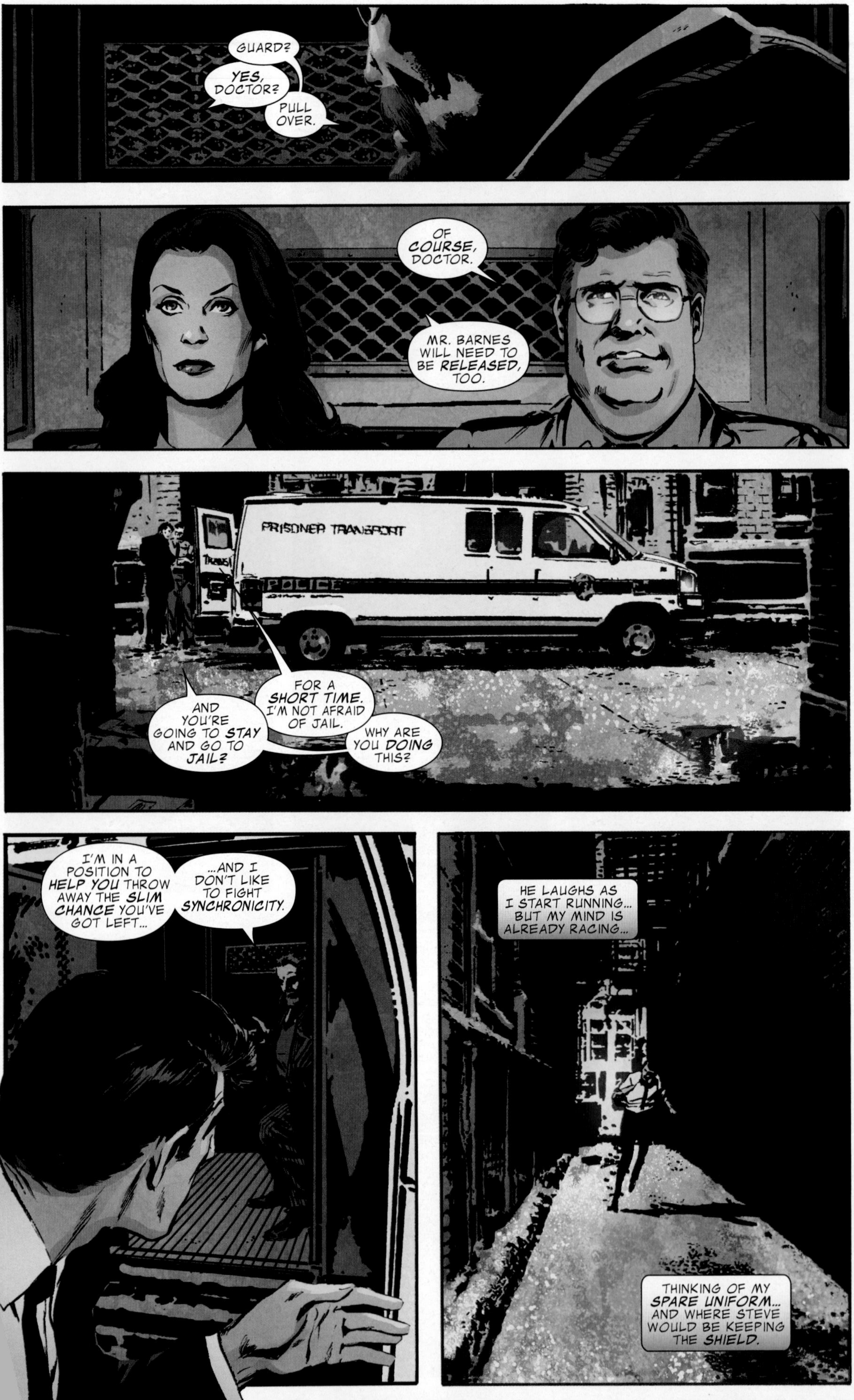
GUARD?
*YES,* DOCTOR?
PULL OVER.
OF *COURSE,* DOCTOR.
MR. BARNES WILL NEED TO BE *RELEASED,* TOO.
PRISONER TRANSPORT
POLICE
AND YOU'RE GOING TO *STAY* AND GO TO *JAIL?*
FOR A *SHORT TIME.* I'M NOT AFRAID OF JAIL.
WHY ARE YOU *DOING* THIS?
I'M IN A POSITION TO *HELP YOU* THROW AWAY THE *SLIM CHANCE* YOU'VE GOT LEFT...
...AND I DON'T LIKE TO FIGHT *SYNCHRONICITY.*
HE LAUGHS AS I START RUNNING... BUT MY MIND IS ALREADY RACING...
THINKING OF MY *SPARE UNIFORM*... AND WHERE STEVE WOULD BE KEEPING THE *SHIELD.*

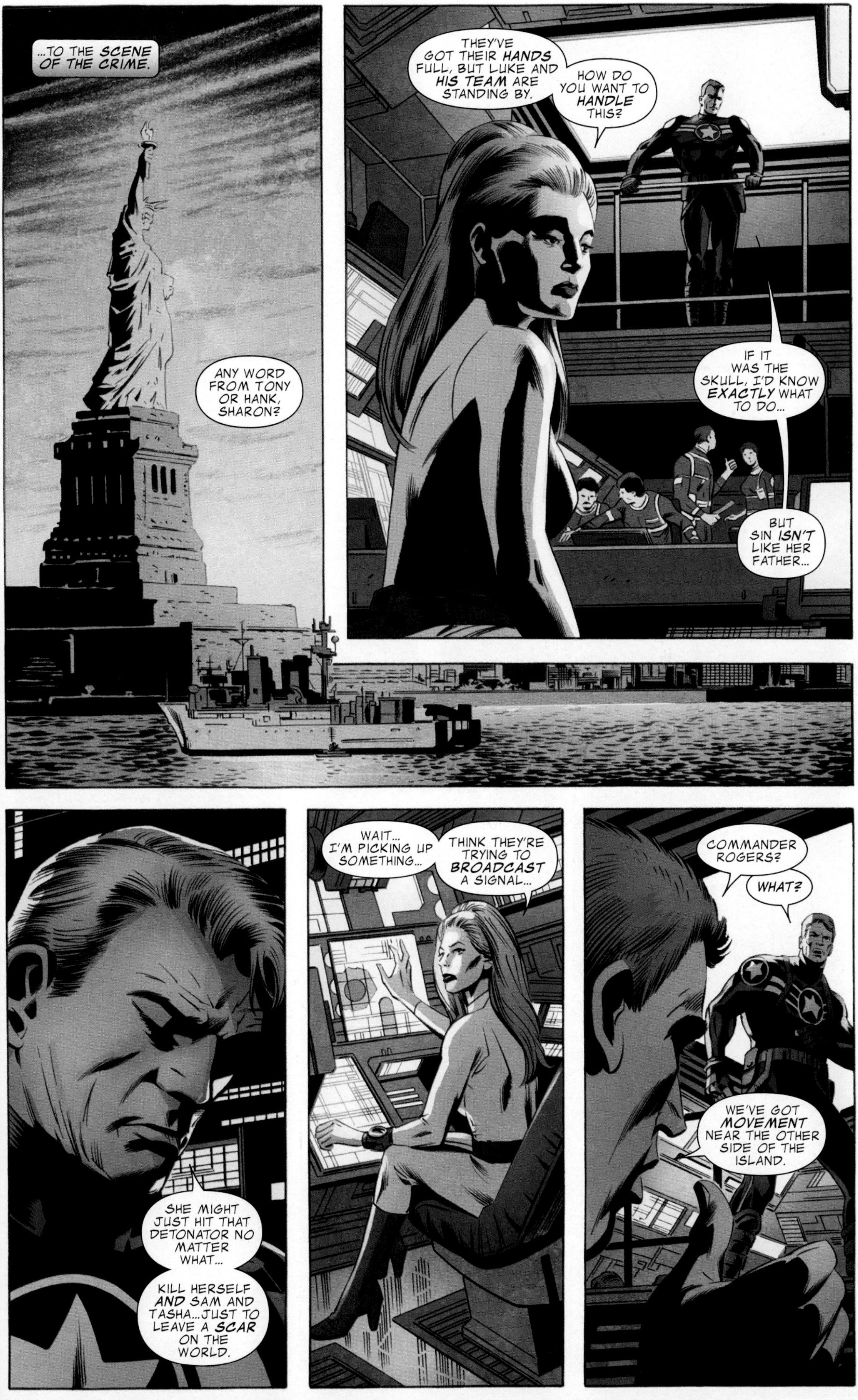
...TO THE SCENE OF THE CRIME.
ANY WORD FROM TONY OR HANK, SHARON?
THEY'VE GOT THEIR HANDS FULL, BUT LUKE AND HIS TEAM ARE STANDING BY.
HOW DO YOU WANT TO HANDLE THIS?
IF IT WAS THE SKULL, I'D KNOW EXACTLY WHAT TO DO...
BUT SIN ISN'T LIKE HER FATHER...
SHE MIGHT JUST HIT THAT DETONATOR NO MATTER WHAT...
KILL HERSELF AND SAM AND TASHA...JUST TO LEAVE A SCAR ON THE WORLD.
WAIT... I'M PICKING UP SOMETHING...
THINK THEY'RE TRYING TO BROADCAST A SIGNAL...
COMMANDER ROGERS?
WHAT?
WE'VE GOT MOVEMENT NEAR THE OTHER SIDE OF THE ISLAND.

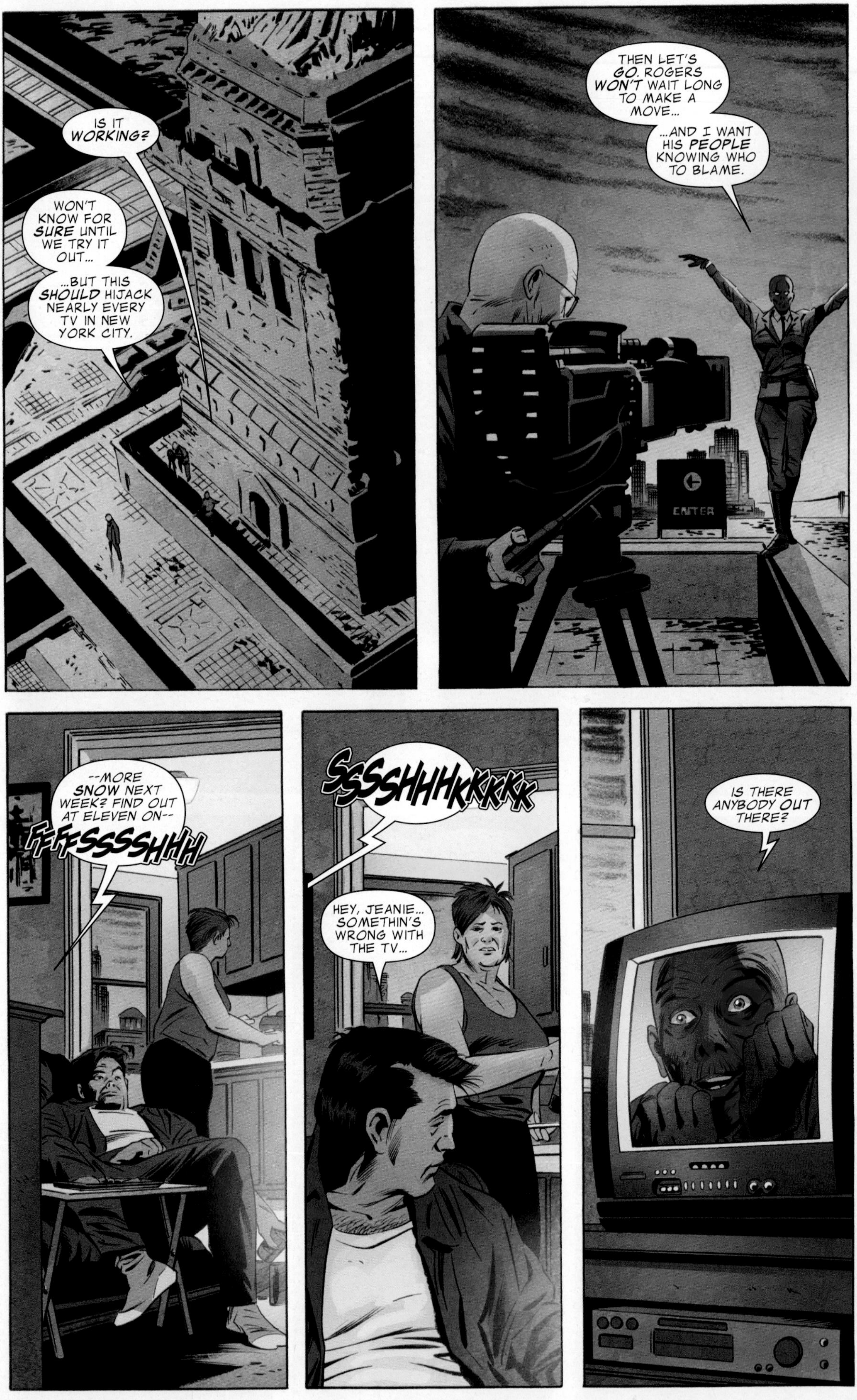
IS IT WORKING?
WON'T KNOW FOR SURE UNTIL WE TRY IT OUT...
...BUT THIS SHOULD HIJACK NEARLY EVERY TV IN NEW YORK CITY.
THEN LET'S GO. ROGERS WON'T WAIT LONG TO MAKE A MOVE...
...AND I WANT HIS PEOPLE KNOWING WHO TO BLAME.
ENTER
--MORE SNOW NEXT WEEK? FIND OUT AT ELEVEN ON--
FFFFSSSSSHHH
SSSSHHHKKKKK
HEY, JEANIE... SOMETHIN'S WRONG WITH THE TV...
IS THERE ANYBODY OUT THERE?

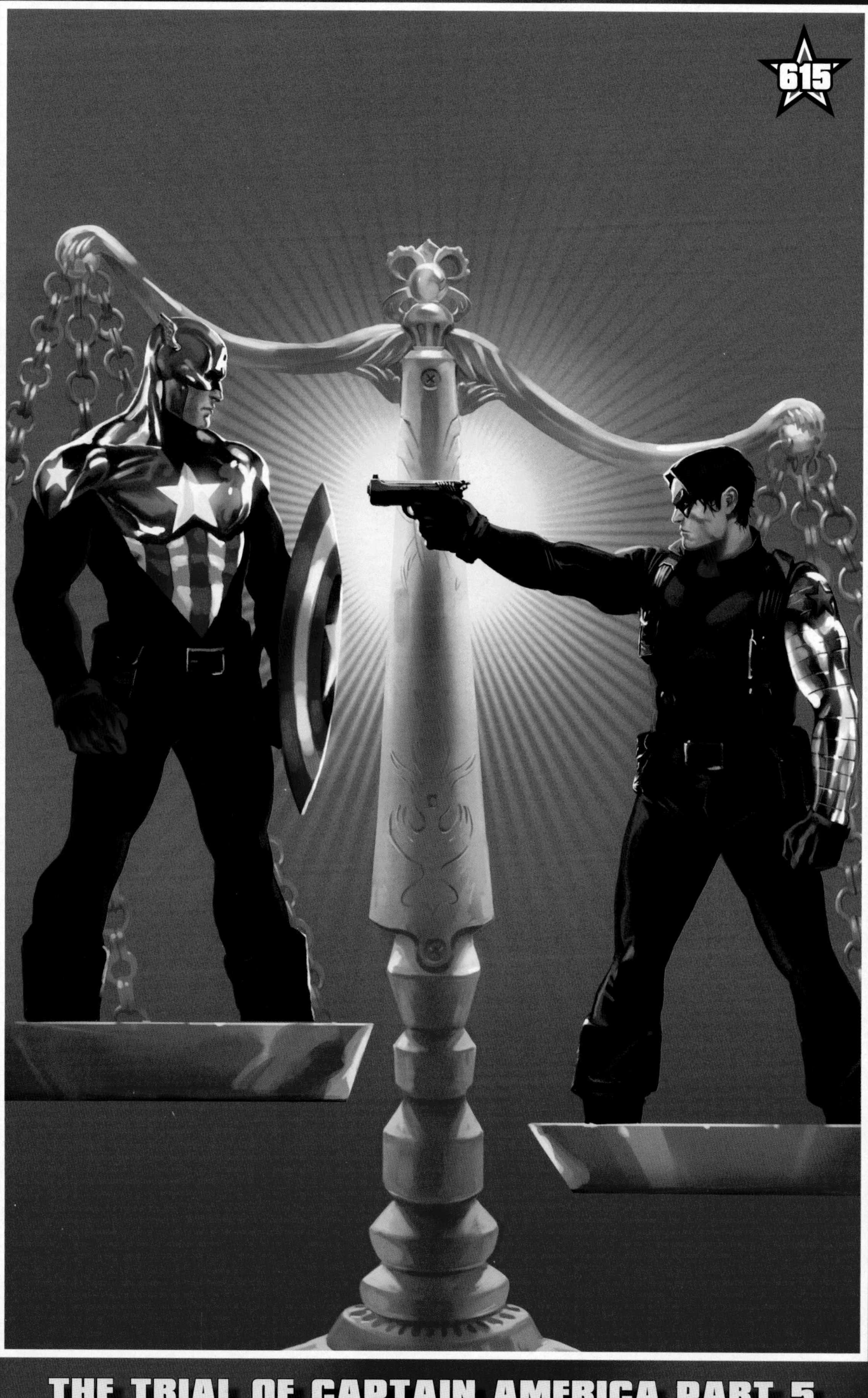
615

# THE TRIAL OF CAPTAIN AMERICA PART 5

OKAY...HE'S FASTER, TOO.

YOU'RE A *FOOL*...AND I WILL TEAR YOUR *ENTRAILS* FROM YOUR--

--GUHH--

GOTTA REMEMBER TO THANK STARK FOR DOING SUCH A GOOD JOB ON THE IMPACT RESISTANCE IN THIS UNIFORM.

THINK IT JUST SAVED MY LIFE.

OR KEPT ME GOING LONG ENOUGH FOR BACKUP TO ARRIVE, AT LEAST.

KA-WAAAM

OKAY... SHAKE IT OFF, BUCK...

GET YOUR BEARINGS.

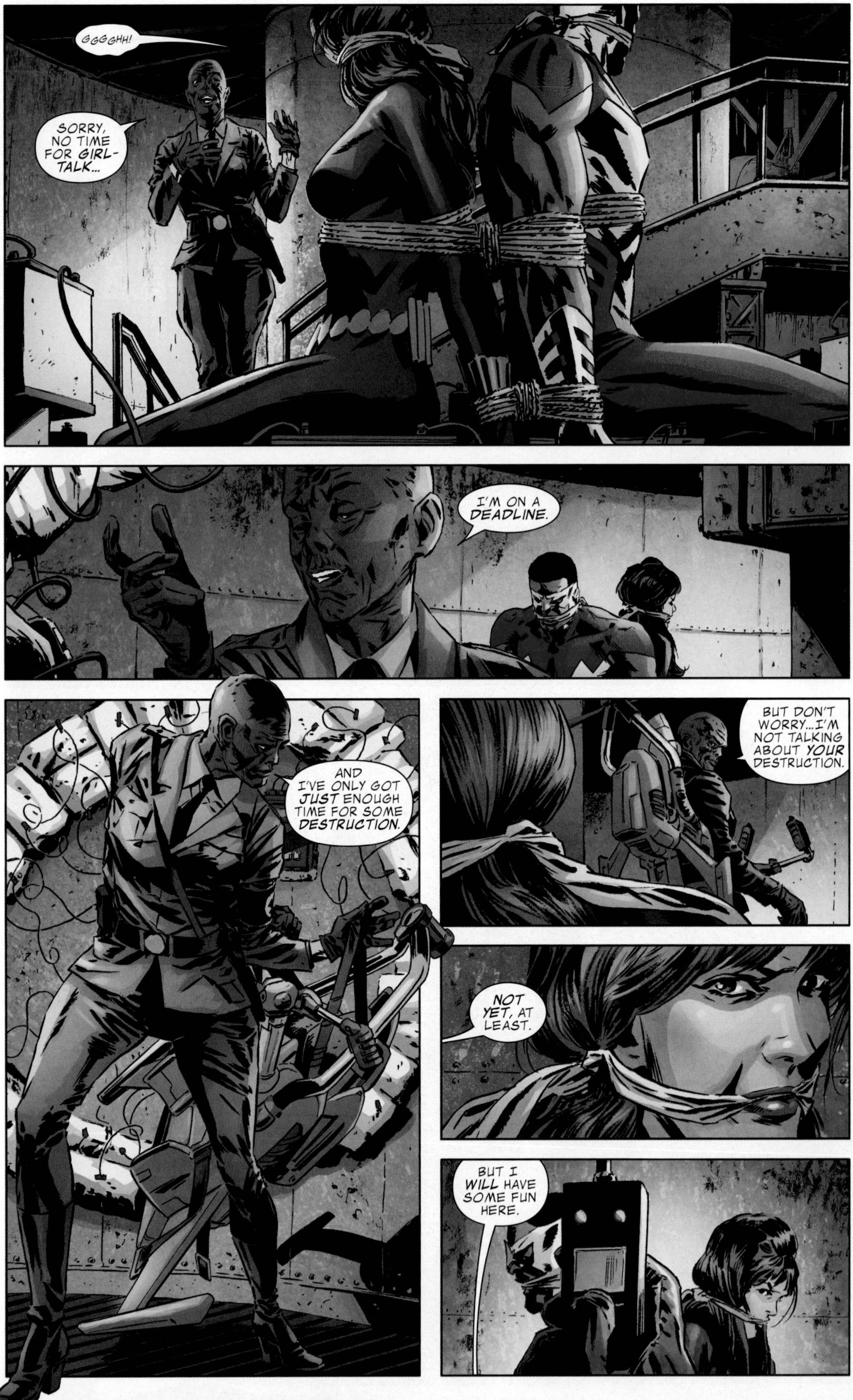
GGGGHH!
SORRY, NO TIME FOR GIRL-TALK...
I'M ON A DEADLINE.
AND I'VE ONLY GOT JUST ENOUGH TIME FOR SOME DESTRUCTION.
BUT DON'T WORRY...I'M NOT TALKING ABOUT YOUR DESTRUCTION.
NOT YET, AT LEAST.
BUT I WILL HAVE SOME FUN HERE.

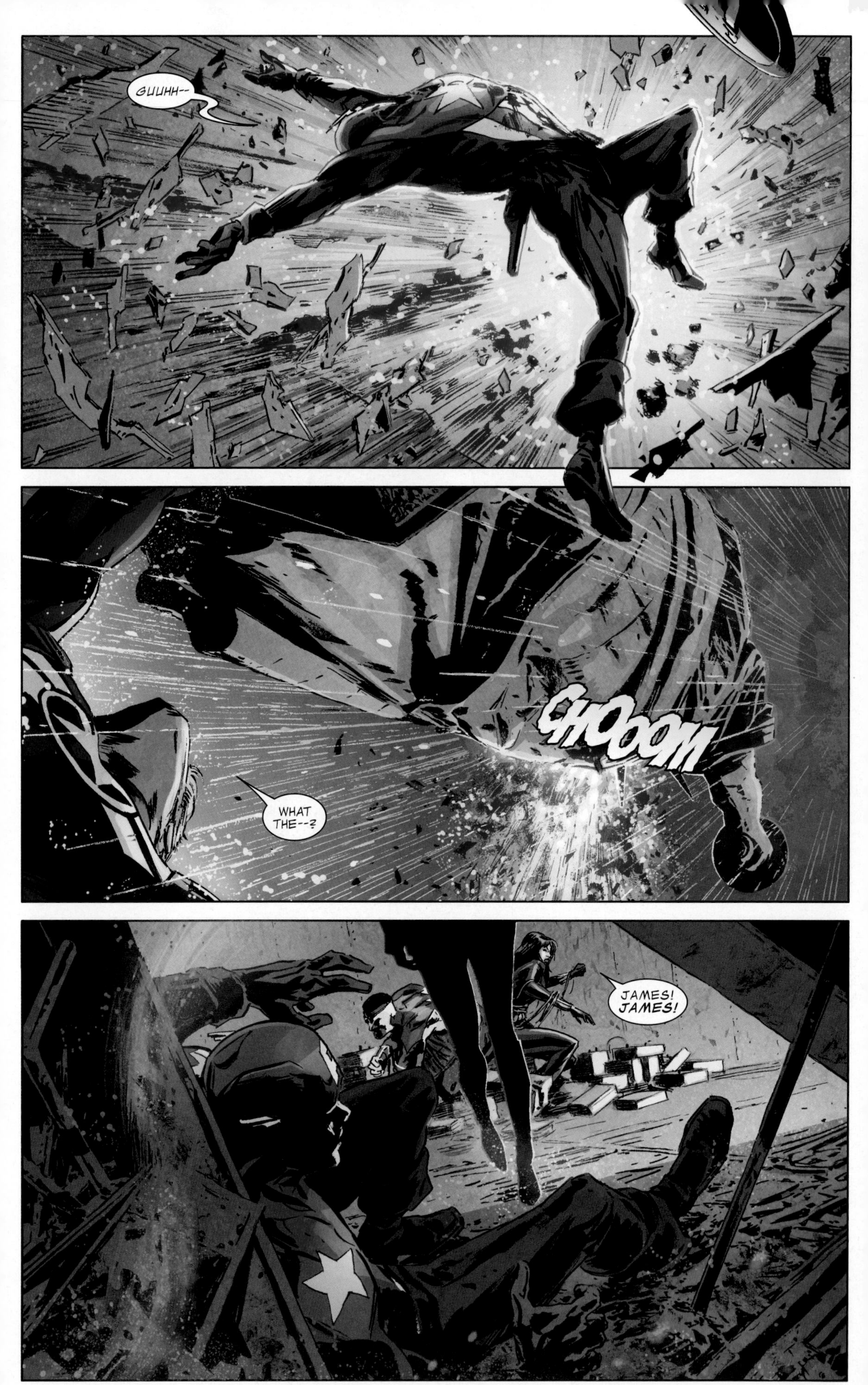
GUUHH--
CHOOOM
WHAT THE--?
JAMES! JAMES!

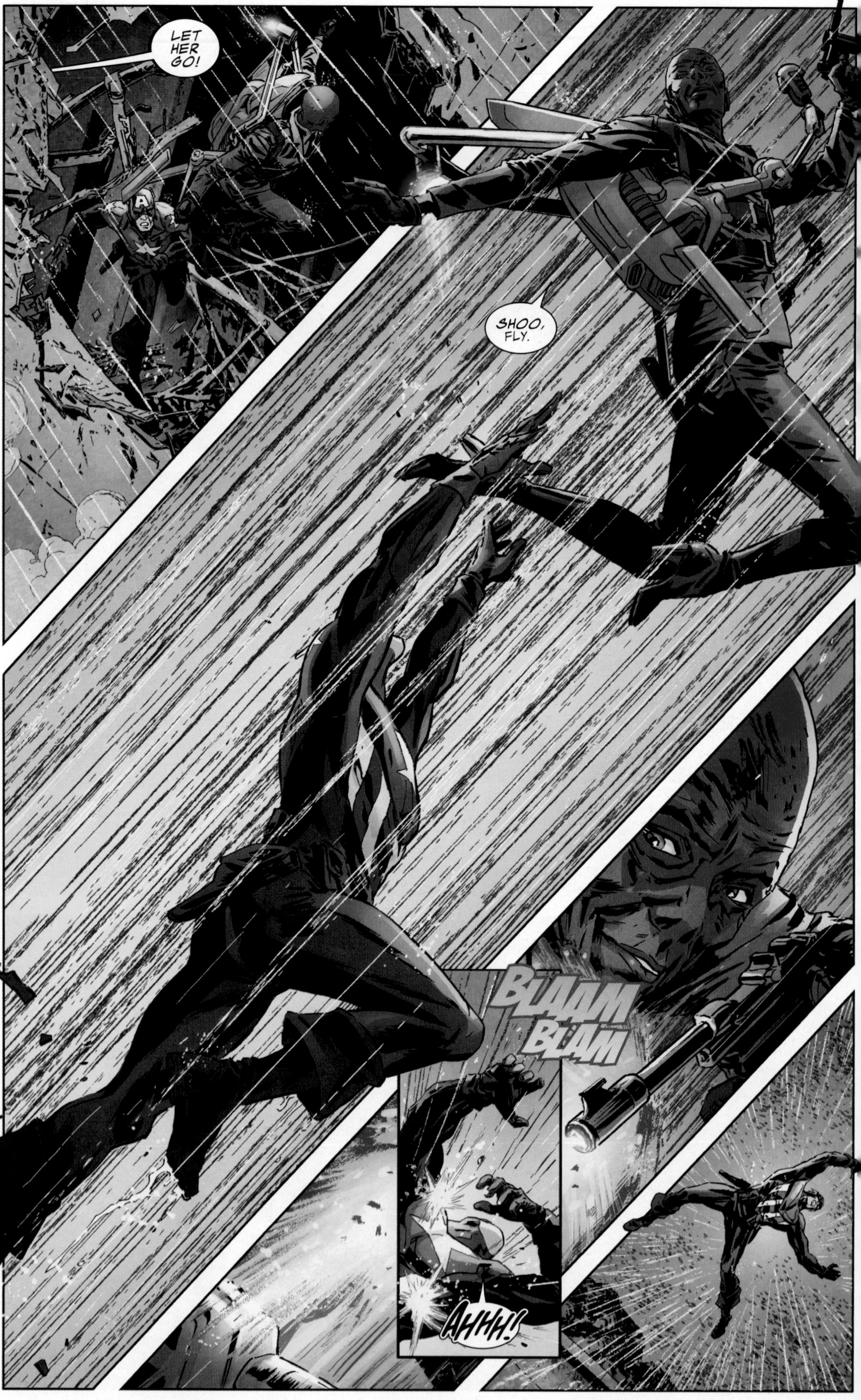
LET HER GO!
SHOO, FLY.
BLAAM
BLAM
AHHH!

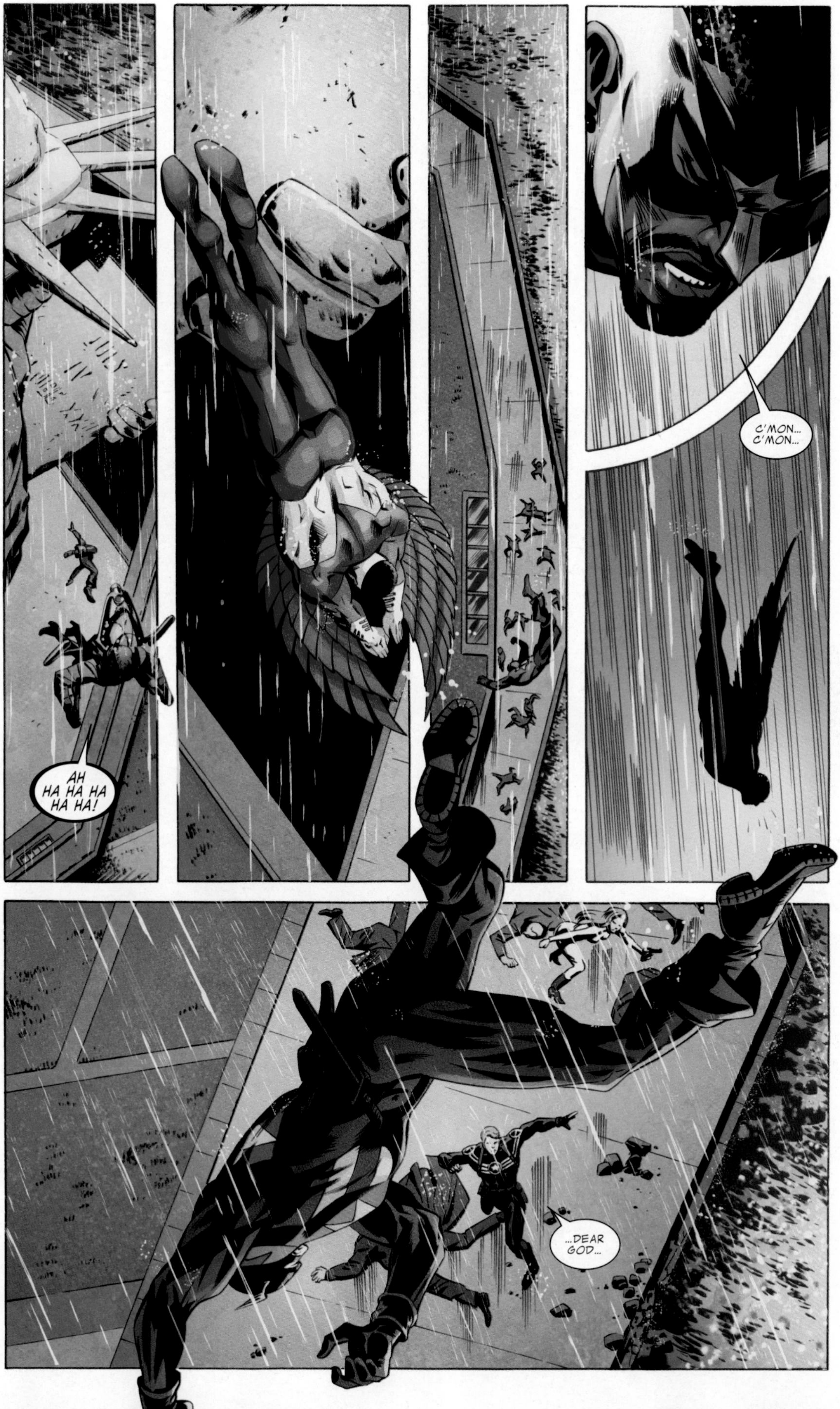
AH
HA HA HA
HA HA!
C'MON...
C'MON...
...DEAR
GOD...

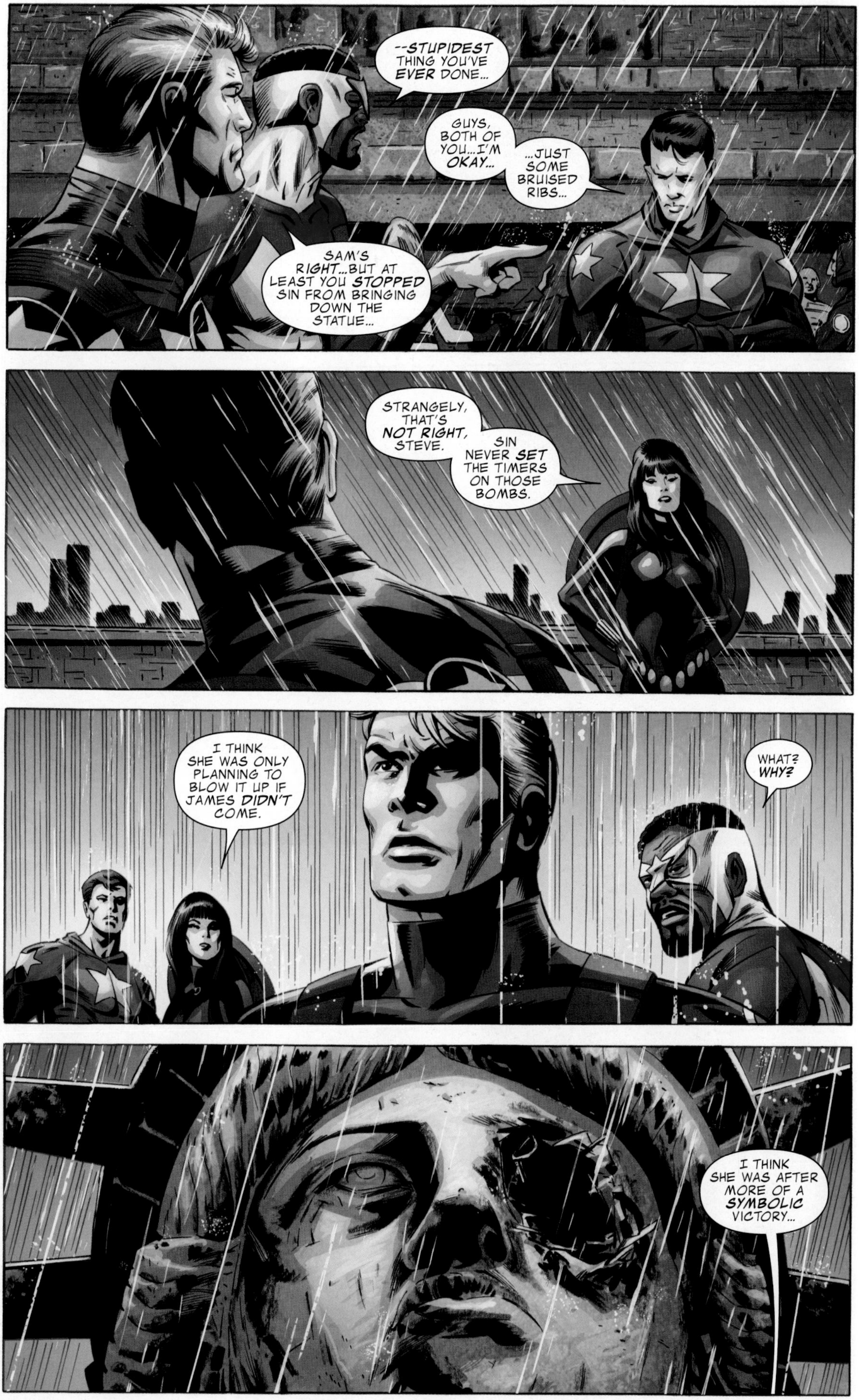
--STUPIDEST THING YOU'VE EVER DONE...
GUYS, BOTH OF YOU...I'M OKAY...
...JUST SOME BRUISED RIBS...
SAM'S RIGHT...BUT AT LEAST YOU STOPPED SIN FROM BRINGING DOWN THE STATUE...
STRANGELY, THAT'S NOT RIGHT, STEVE.
SIN NEVER SET THE TIMERS ON THOSE BOMBS.
I THINK SHE WAS ONLY PLANNING TO BLOW IT UP IF JAMES DIDN'T COME.
WHAT? WHY?
I THINK SHE WAS AFTER MORE OF A SYMBOLIC VICTORY...

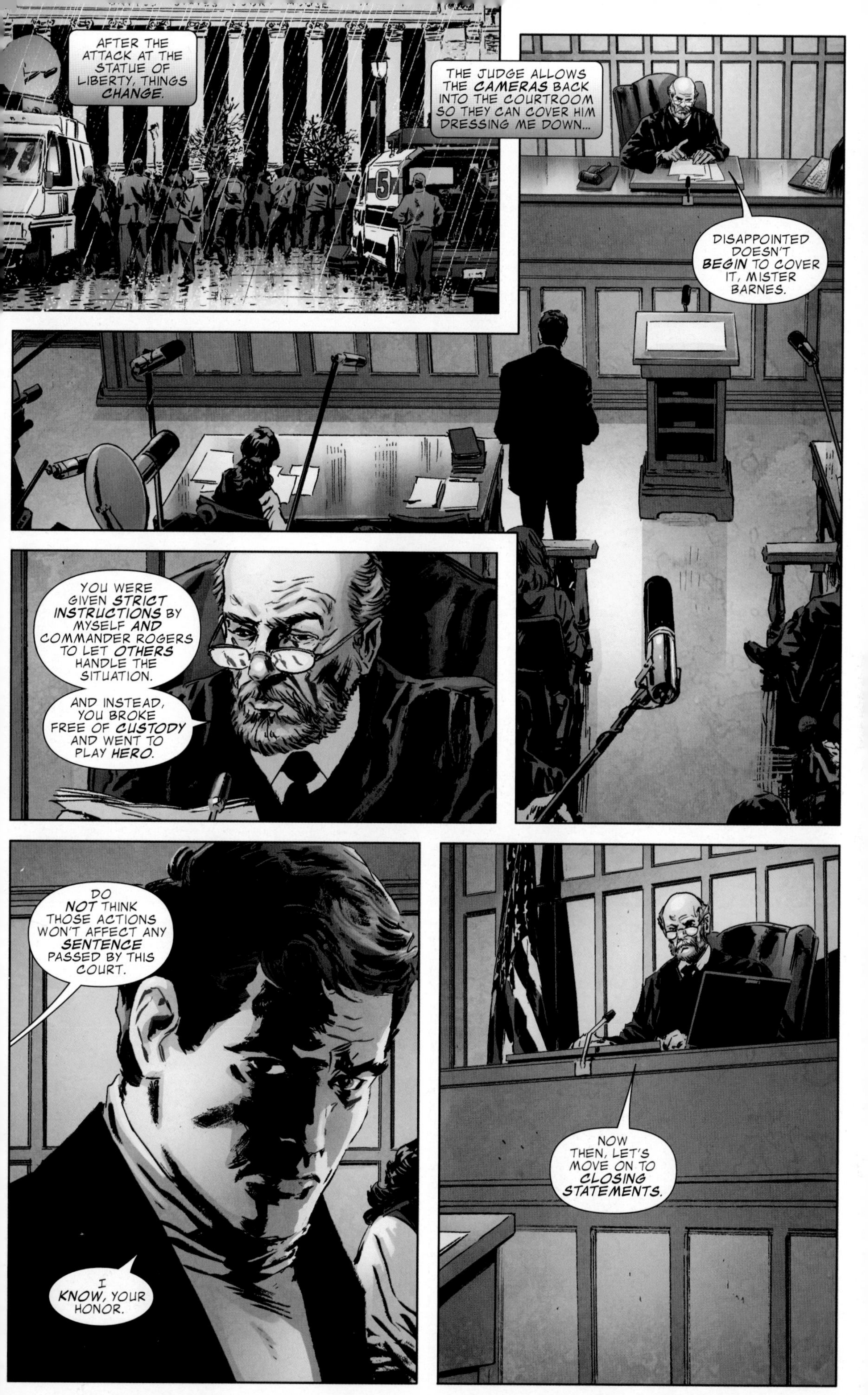
AFTER THE ATTACK AT THE STATUE OF LIBERTY, THINGS CHANGE.
THE JUDGE ALLOWS THE CAMERAS BACK INTO THE COURTROOM SO THEY CAN COVER HIM DRESSING ME DOWN...
DISAPPOINTED DOESN'T BEGIN TO COVER IT, MISTER BARNES.
YOU WERE GIVEN STRICT INSTRUCTIONS BY MYSELF AND COMMANDER ROGERS TO LET OTHERS HANDLE THE SITUATION.
AND INSTEAD, YOU BROKE FREE OF CUSTODY AND WENT TO PLAY HERO.
DO NOT THINK THOSE ACTIONS WON'T AFFECT ANY SENTENCE PASSED BY THIS COURT.
I KNOW, YOUR HONOR.
NOW THEN, LET'S MOVE ON TO CLOSING STATEMENTS.

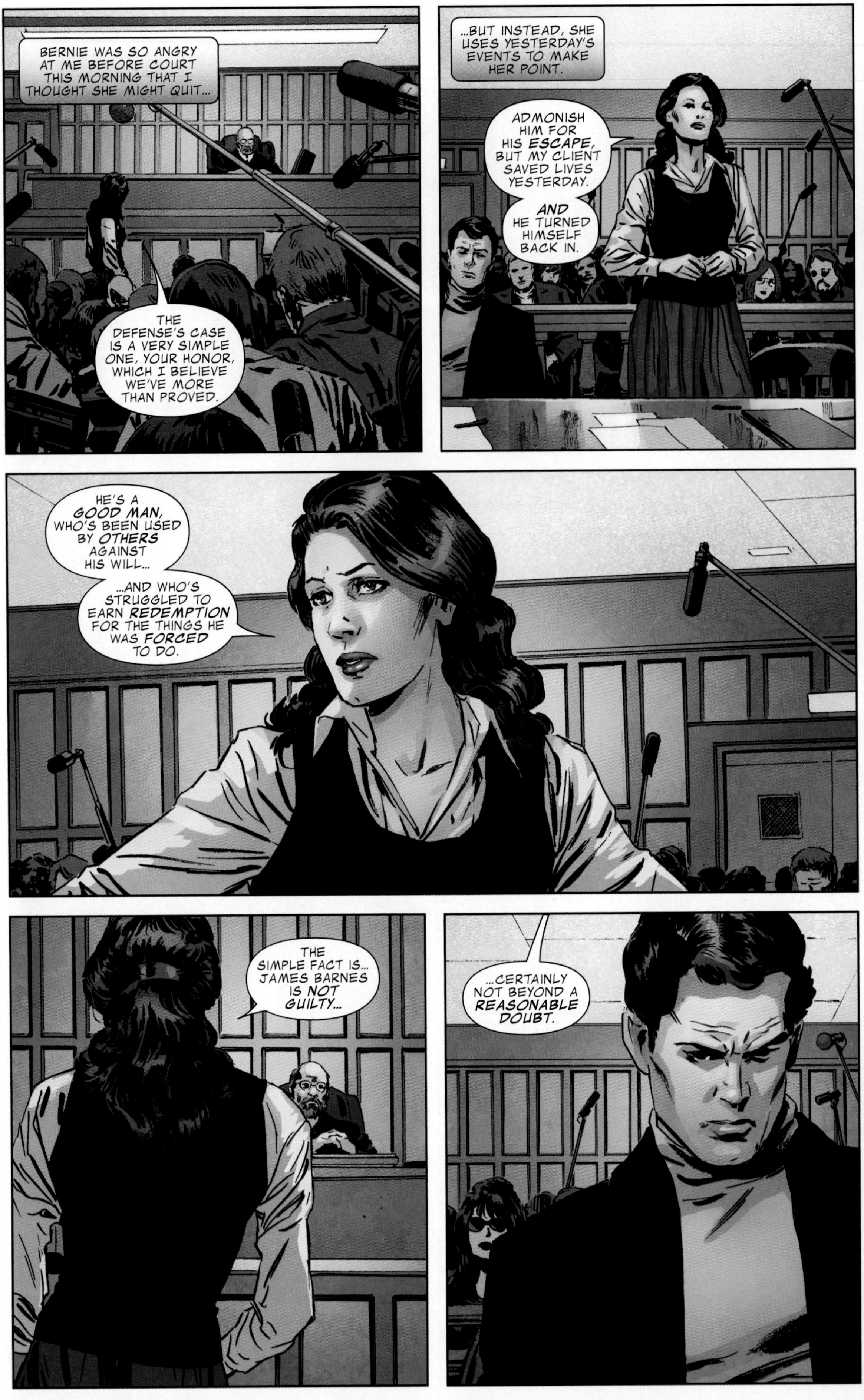
BERNIE WAS SO ANGRY AT ME BEFORE COURT THIS MORNING THAT I THOUGHT SHE MIGHT QUIT...
THE DEFENSE'S CASE IS A VERY SIMPLE ONE, YOUR HONOR, WHICH I BELIEVE WE'VE MORE THAN PROVED.
...BUT INSTEAD, SHE USES YESTERDAY'S EVENTS TO MAKE HER POINT.
ADMONISH HIM FOR HIS ESCAPE, BUT MY CLIENT SAVED LIVES YESTERDAY.
AND HE TURNED HIMSELF BACK IN.
HE'S A GOOD MAN, WHO'S BEEN USED BY OTHERS AGAINST HIS WILL...
...AND WHO'S STRUGGLED TO EARN REDEMPTION FOR THE THINGS HE WAS FORCED TO DO.
THE SIMPLE FACT IS... JAMES BARNES IS NOT GUILTY...
...CERTAINLY NOT BEYOND A REASONABLE DOUBT.

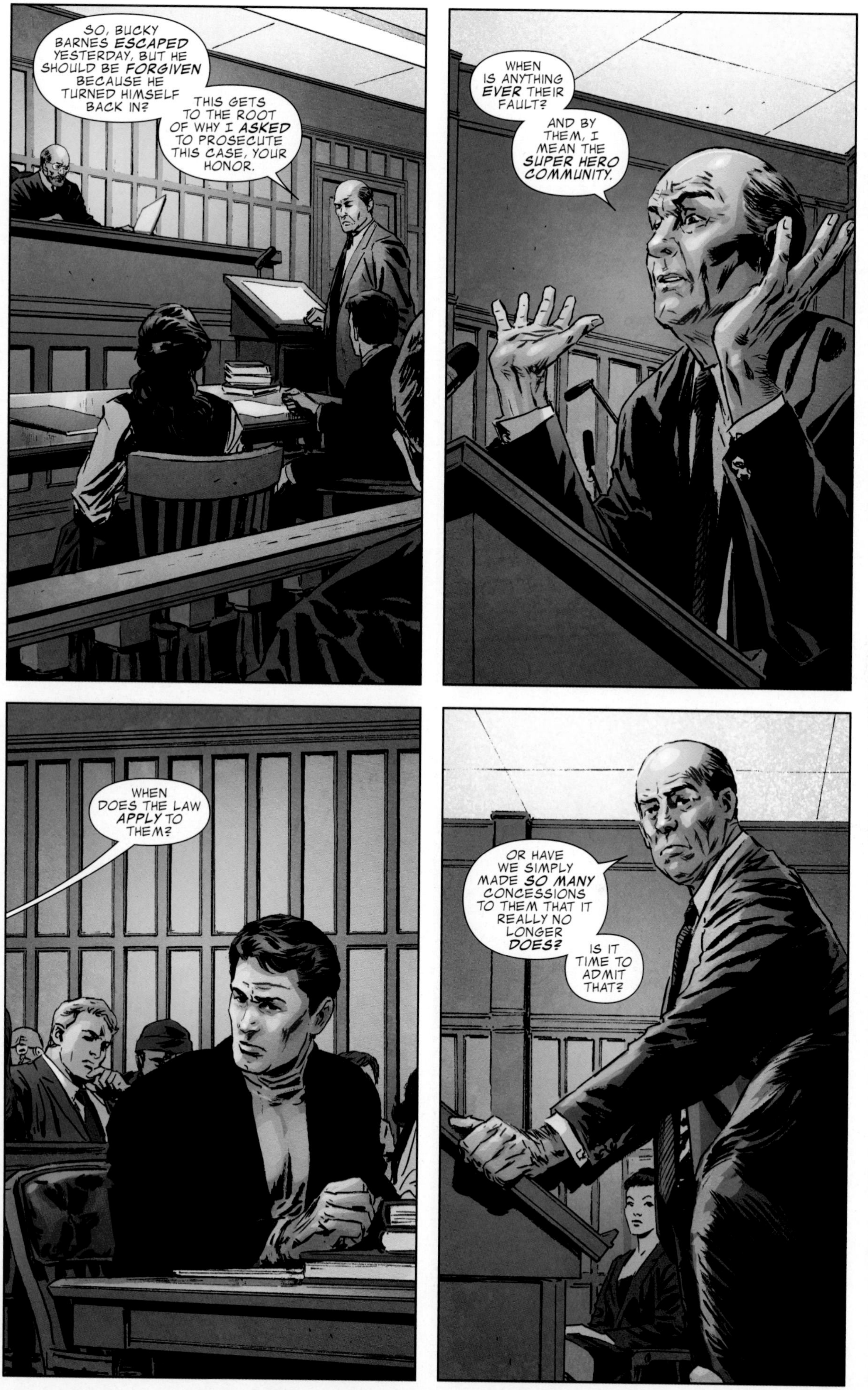
SO, BUCKY BARNES ESCAPED YESTERDAY, BUT HE SHOULD BE FORGIVEN BECAUSE HE TURNED HIMSELF BACK IN?
THIS GETS TO THE ROOT OF WHY I ASKED TO PROSECUTE THIS CASE, YOUR HONOR.
WHEN IS ANYTHING EVER THEIR FAULT?
AND BY THEM, I MEAN THE SUPER HERO COMMUNITY.
WHEN DOES THE LAW APPLY TO THEM?
OR HAVE WE SIMPLY MADE SO MANY CONCESSIONS TO THEM THAT IT REALLY NO LONGER DOES?
IS IT TIME TO ADMIT THAT?

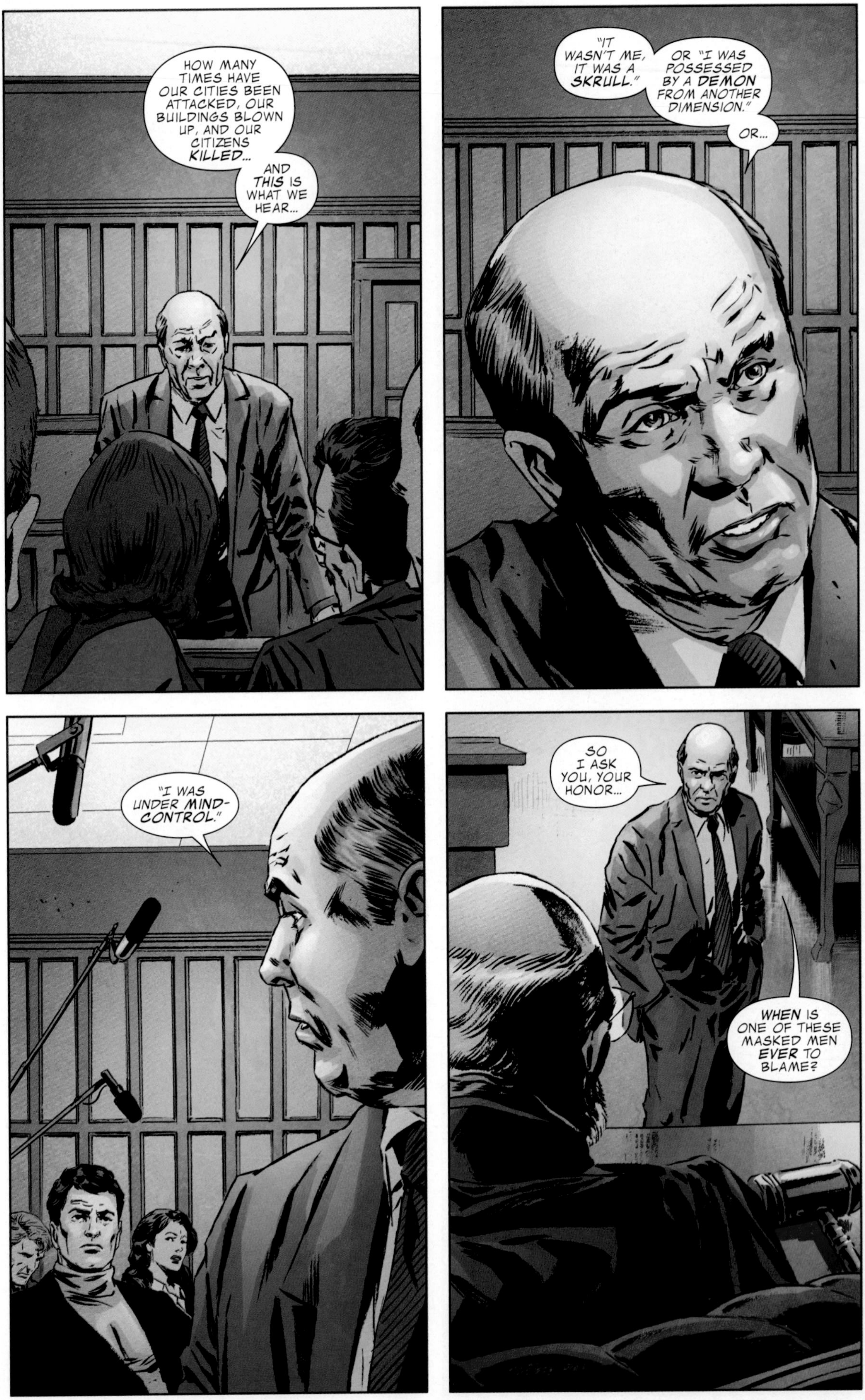
HOW MANY TIMES HAVE OUR CITIES BEEN ATTACKED, OUR BUILDINGS BLOWN UP, AND OUR CITIZENS KILLED...
AND THIS IS WHAT WE HEAR...
"IT WASN'T ME, IT WAS A SKRULL."
OR "I WAS POSSESSED BY A DEMON FROM ANOTHER DIMENSION."
OR...
"I WAS UNDER MIND-CONTROL."
SO I ASK YOU, YOUR HONOR...
WHEN IS ONE OF THESE MASKED MEN EVER TO BLAME?

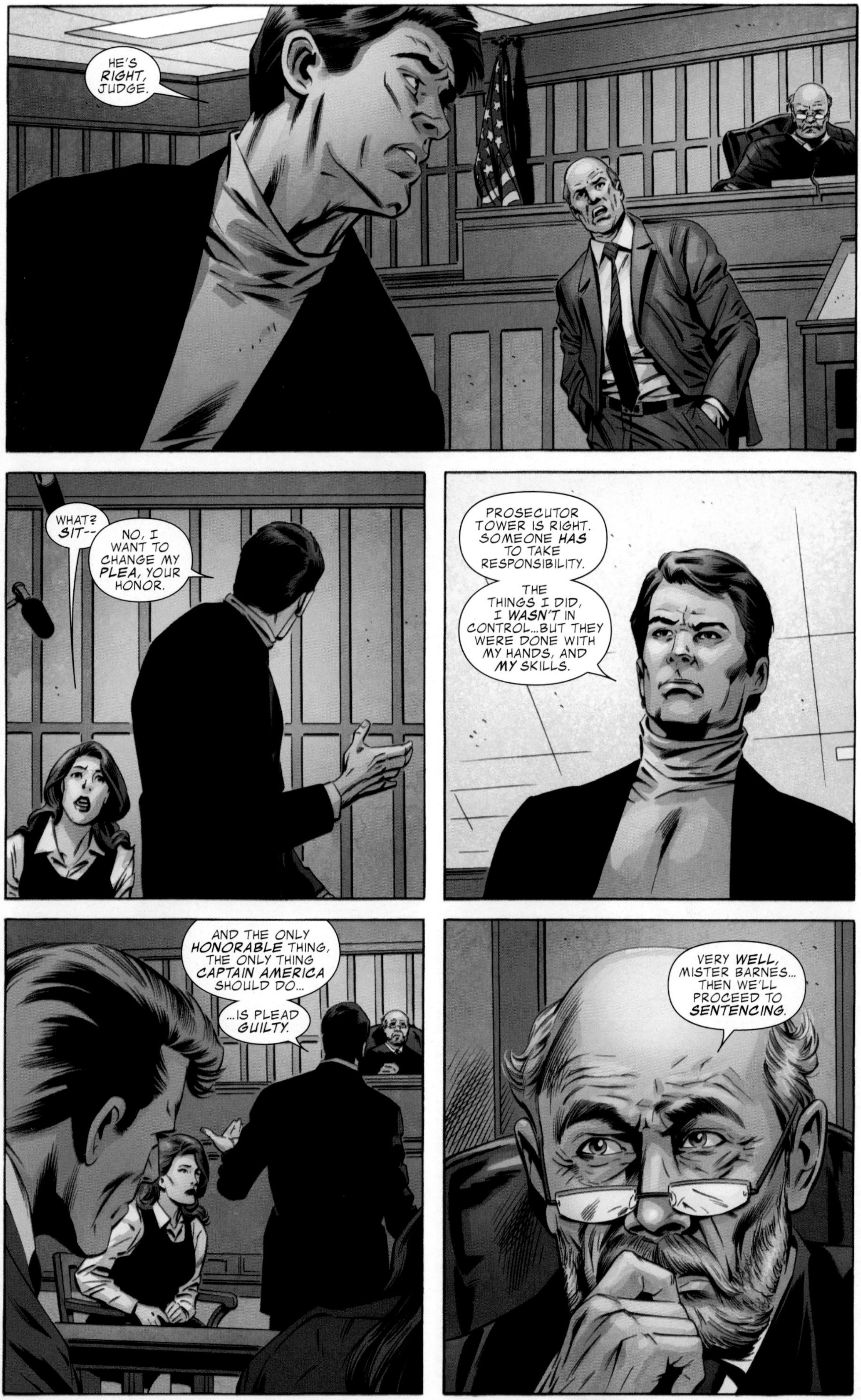
HE'S RIGHT, JUDGE.
WHAT? SIT--
NO, I WANT TO CHANGE MY PLEA, YOUR HONOR.
PROSECUTOR TOWER IS RIGHT. SOMEONE HAS TO TAKE RESPONSIBILITY.
THE THINGS I DID, I WASN'T IN CONTROL...BUT THEY WERE DONE WITH MY HANDS, AND MY SKILLS.
AND THE ONLY HONORABLE THING, THE ONLY THING CAPTAIN AMERICA SHOULD DO...
...IS PLEAD GUILTY.
VERY WELL, MISTER BARNES... THEN WE'LL PROCEED TO SENTENCING.

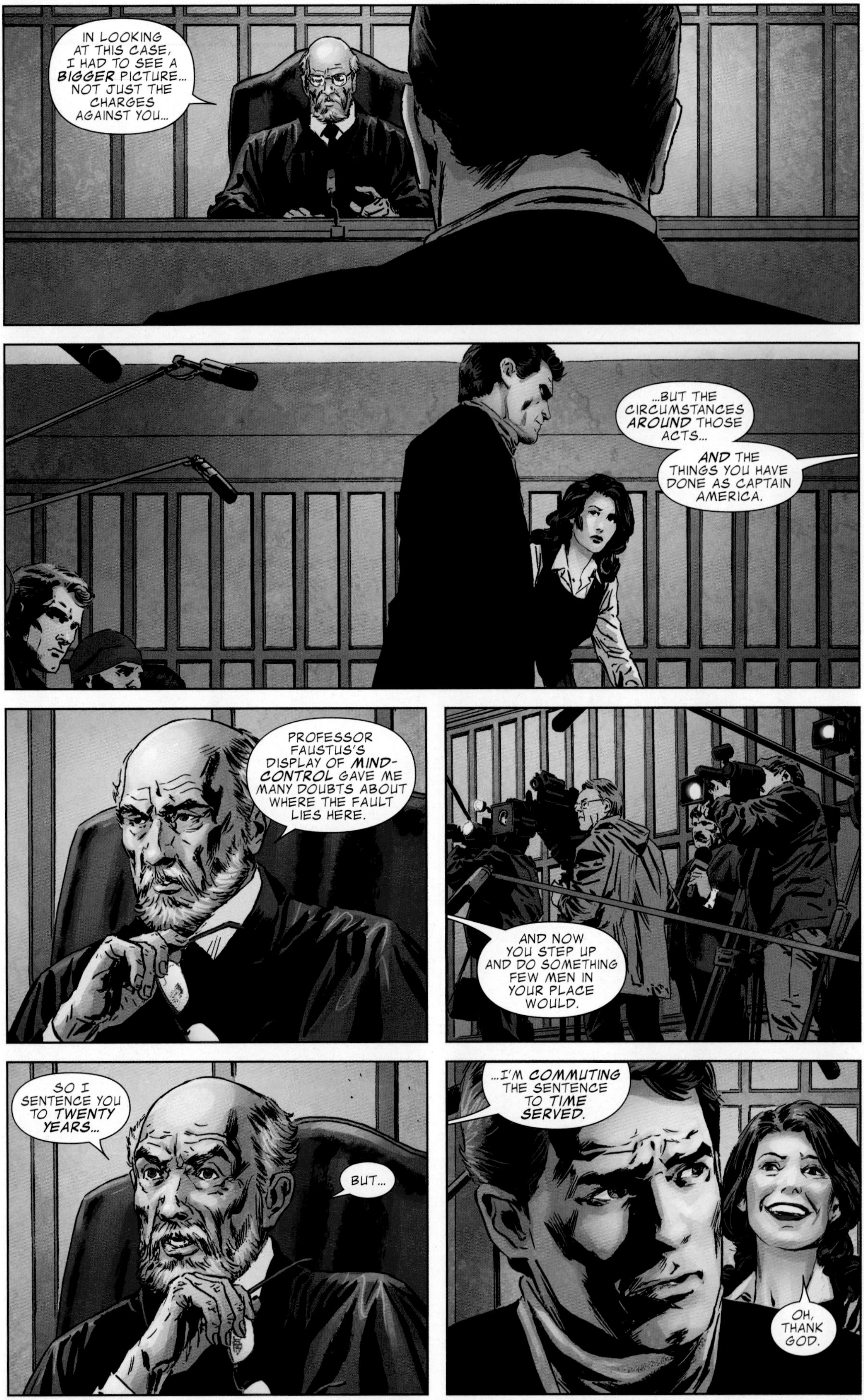
IN LOOKING AT THIS CASE, I HAD TO SEE A BIGGER PICTURE... NOT JUST THE CHARGES AGAINST YOU...
...BUT THE CIRCUMSTANCES AROUND THOSE ACTS...
AND THE THINGS YOU HAVE DONE AS CAPTAIN AMERICA.
PROFESSOR FAUSTUS'S DISPLAY OF MIND-CONTROL GAVE ME MANY DOUBTS ABOUT WHERE THE FAULT LIES HERE.
AND NOW YOU STEP UP AND DO SOMETHING FEW MEN IN YOUR PLACE WOULD.
SO I SENTENCE YOU TO TWENTY YEARS...
BUT...
...I'M COMMUTING THE SENTENCE TO TIME SERVED.
OH, THANK GOD.

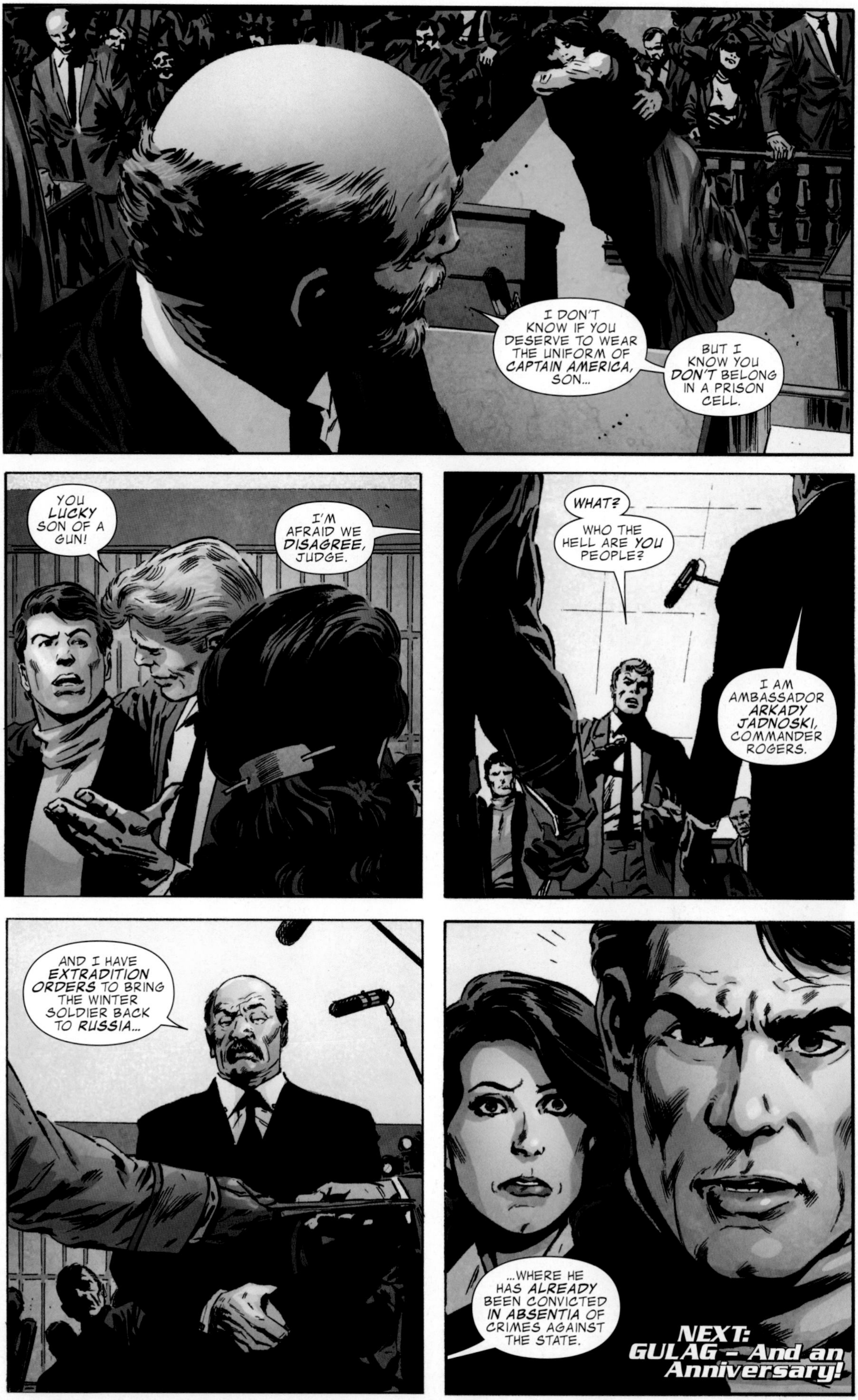
I DON'T KNOW IF YOU DESERVE TO WEAR THE UNIFORM OF CAPTAIN AMERICA, SON...
BUT I KNOW YOU DON'T BELONG IN A PRISON CELL.
YOU LUCKY SON OF A GUN!
I'M AFRAID WE DISAGREE, JUDGE.
WHAT?
WHO THE HELL ARE YOU PEOPLE?
I AM AMBASSADOR ARKADY JADNOSKI, COMMANDER ROGERS.
AND I HAVE EXTRADITION ORDERS TO BRING THE WINTER SOLDIER BACK TO RUSSIA...
...WHERE HE HAS ALREADY BEEN CONVICTED IN ABSENTIA OF CRIMES AGAINST THE STATE.
NEXT: GULAG – And an Anniversary!

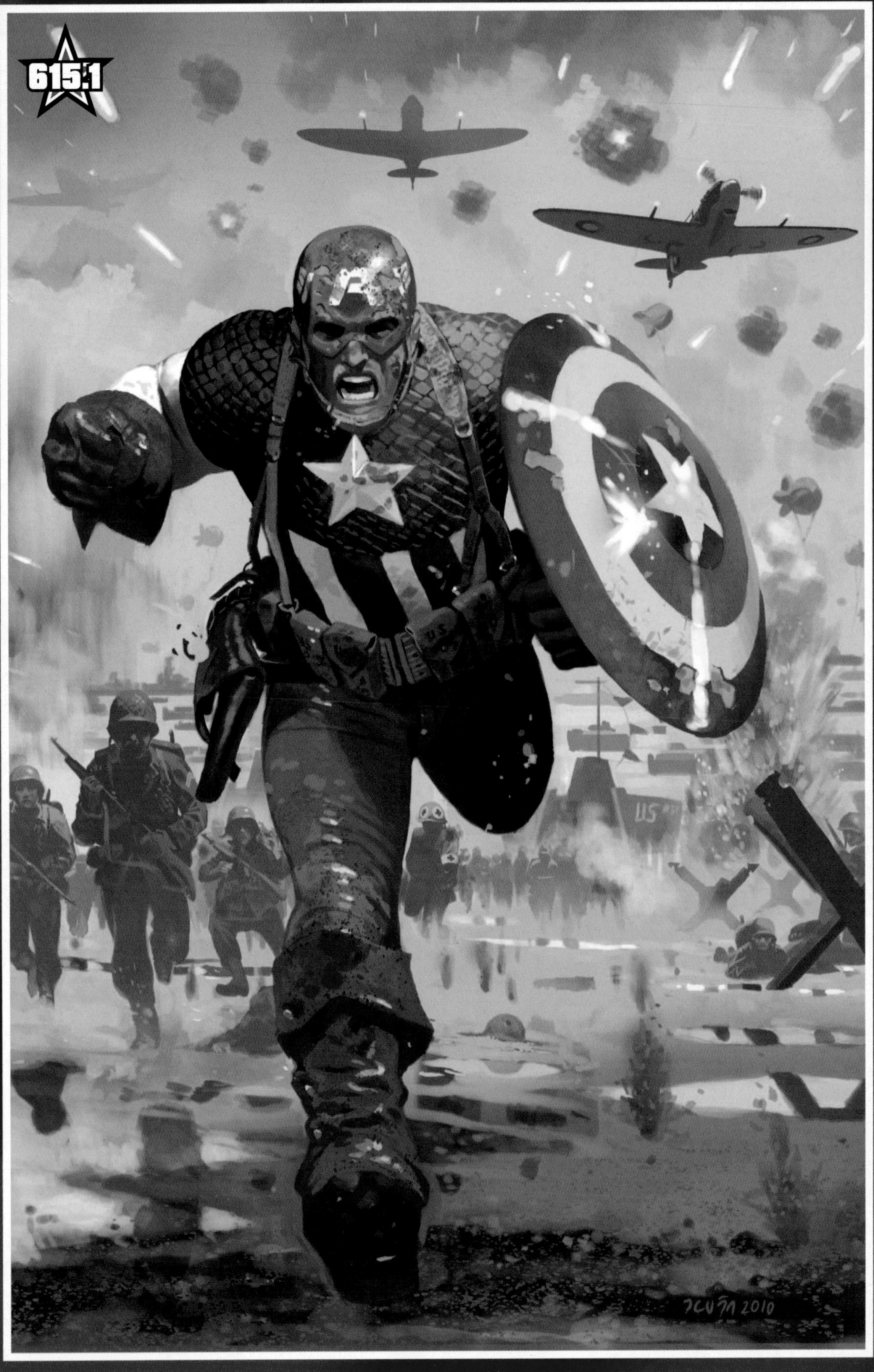
615.1
US
JCNGRN 2010

# AROUND AND ROUND

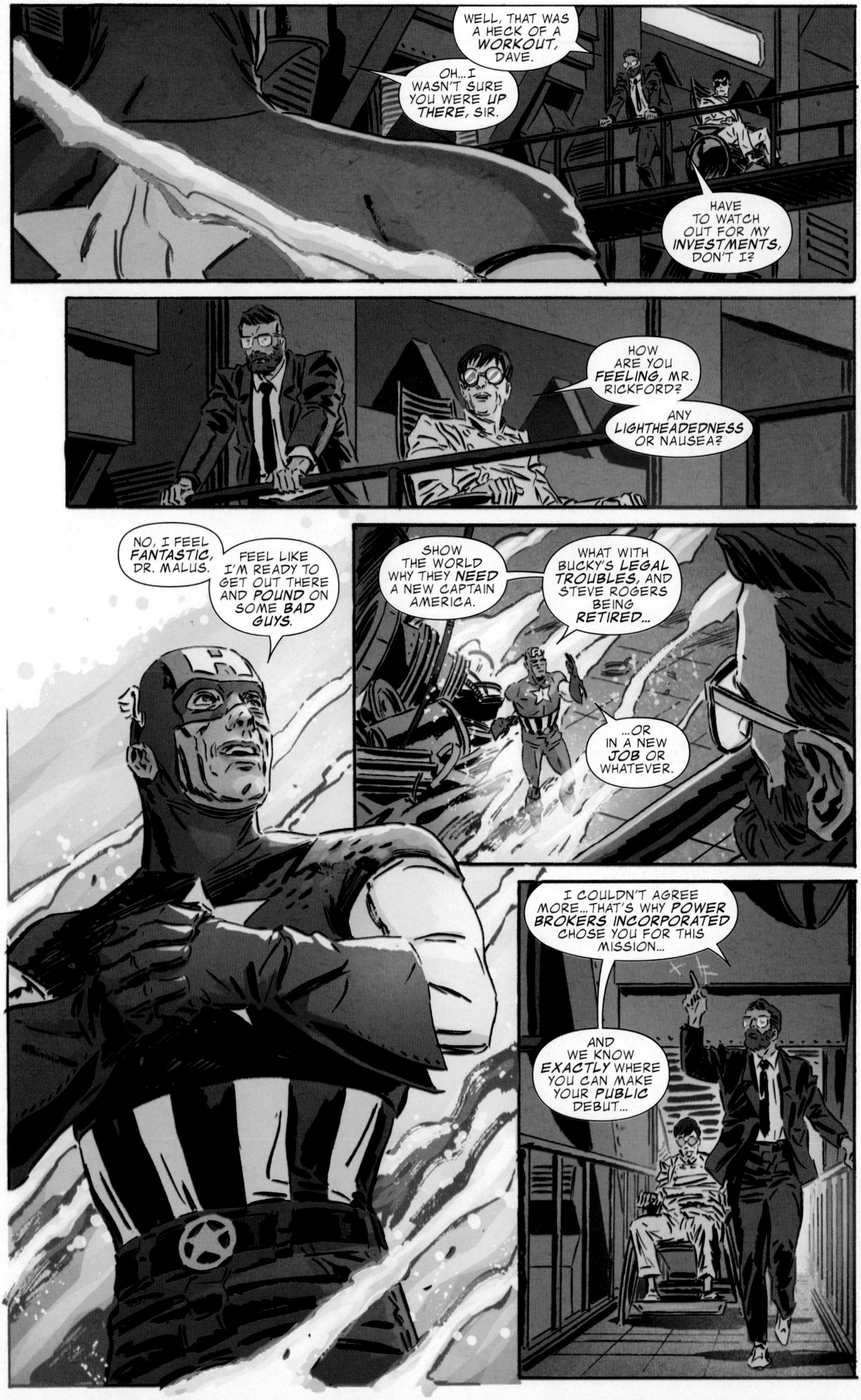
WELL, THAT WAS A HECK OF A WORKOUT, DAVE.
OH... I WASN'T SURE YOU WERE UP THERE, SIR.
HAVE TO WATCH OUT FOR MY INVESTMENTS, DON'T I?
HOW ARE YOU FEELING, MR. RICKFORD?
ANY LIGHTHEADEDNESS OR NAUSEA?
NO, I FEEL FANTASTIC, DR. MALUS.
FEEL LIKE I'M READY TO GET OUT THERE AND POUND ON SOME BAD GUYS.
SHOW THE WORLD WHY THEY NEED A NEW CAPTAIN AMERICA.
WHAT WITH BUCKY'S LEGAL TROUBLES, AND STEVE ROGERS BEING RETIRED...
...OR IN A NEW JOB OR WHATEVER.
I COULDN'T AGREE MORE... THAT'S WHY POWER BROKERS INCORPORATED CHOSE YOU FOR THIS MISSION...
AND WE KNOW EXACTLY WHERE YOU CAN MAKE YOUR PUBLIC DEBUT...

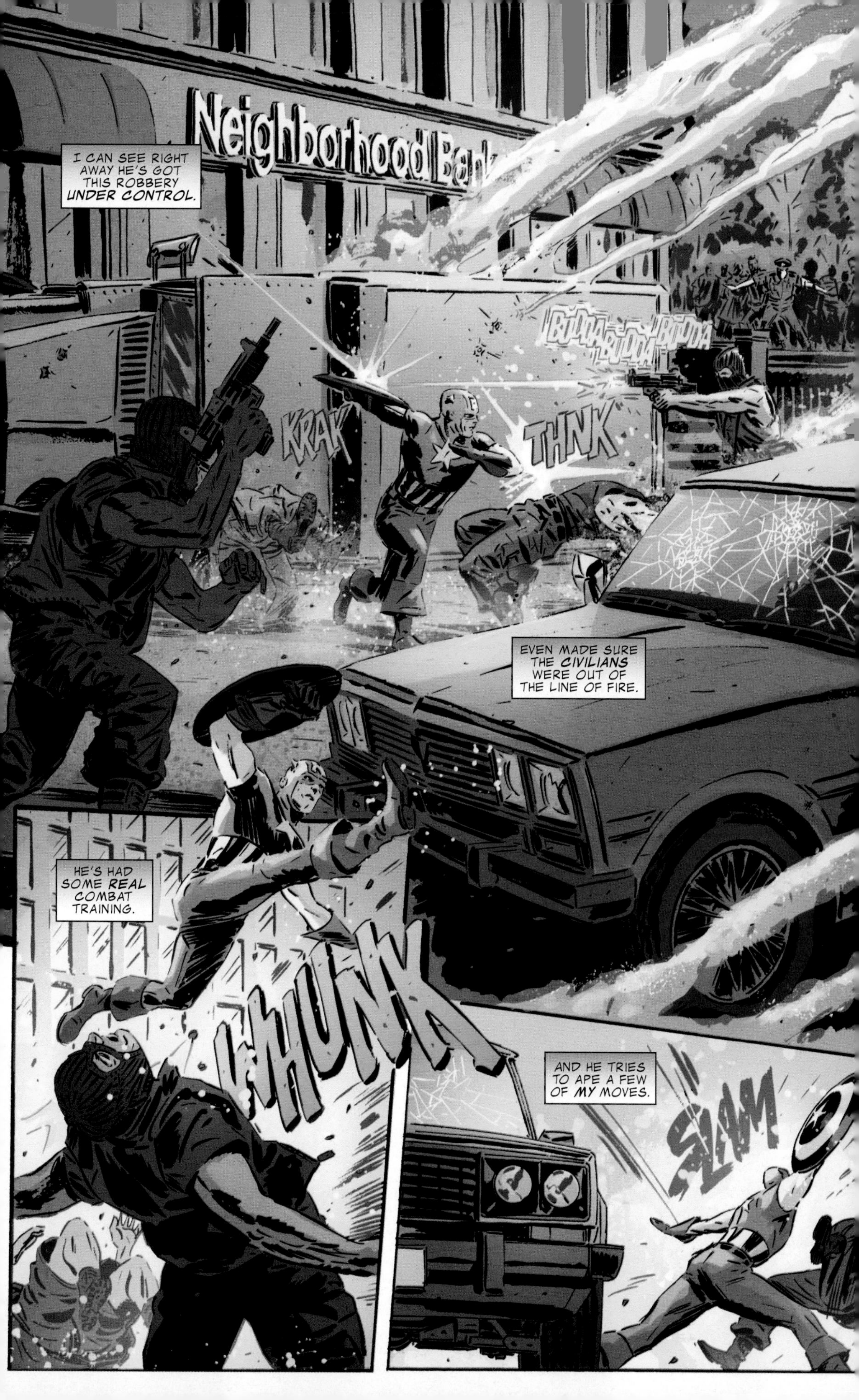
Neighborhood
I CAN SEE RIGHT AWAY HE'S GOT THIS ROBBERY UNDER CONTROL.
BUDDA BUDDA BUDDA
KRAK
THNK
EVEN MADE SURE THE CIVILIANS WERE OUT OF THE LINE OF FIRE.
HE'S HAD SOME REAL COMBAT TRAINING.
AND HE TRIES TO APE A FEW OF MY MOVES.

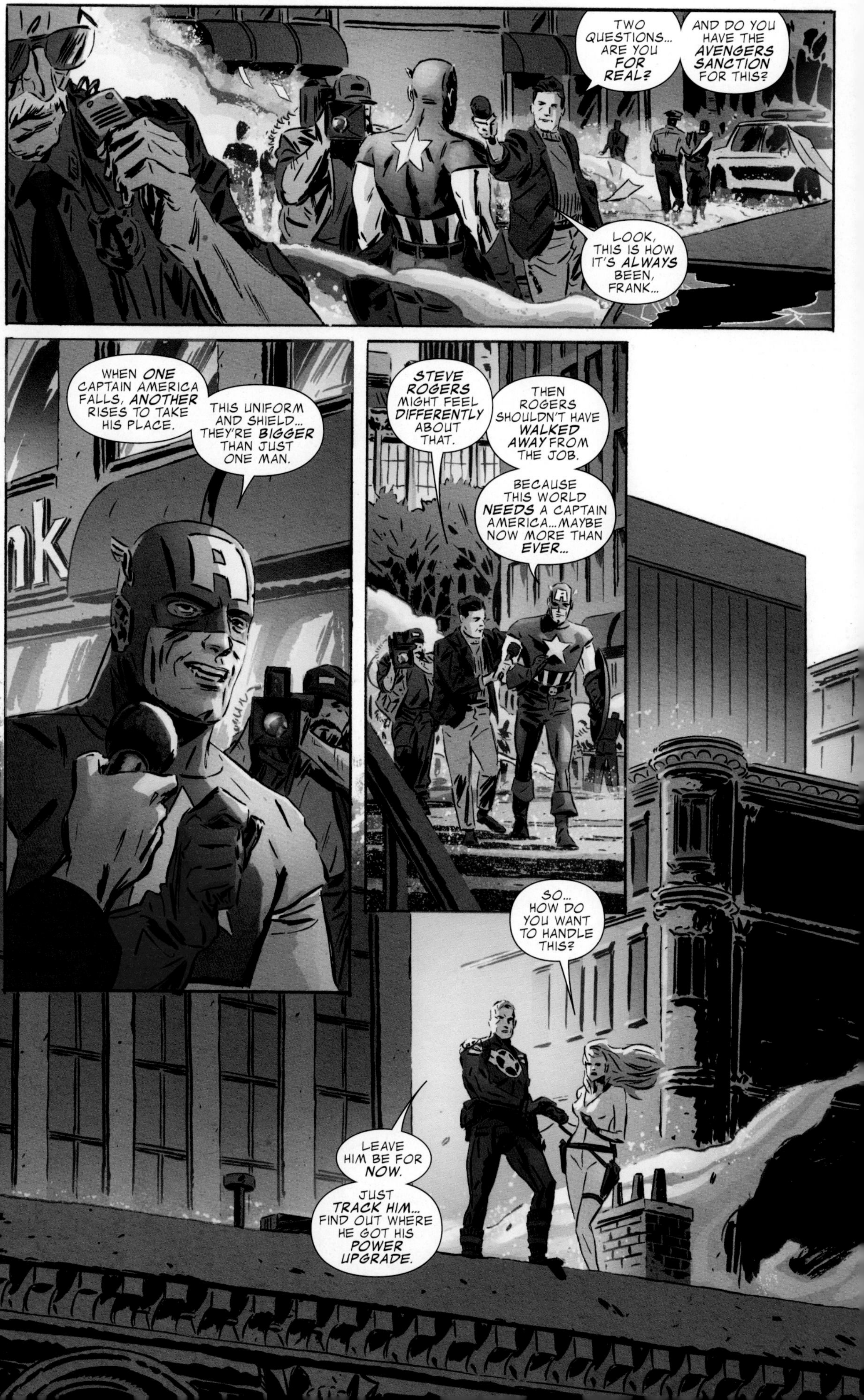
TWO QUESTIONS... ARE YOU FOR REAL?
AND DO YOU HAVE THE AVENGERS SANCTION FOR THIS?
LOOK, THIS IS HOW IT'S ALWAYS BEEN, FRANK...
WHEN ONE CAPTAIN AMERICA FALLS, ANOTHER RISES TO TAKE HIS PLACE.
THIS UNIFORM AND SHIELD... THEY'RE BIGGER THAN JUST ONE MAN.
STEVE ROGERS MIGHT FEEL DIFFERENTLY ABOUT THAT.
THEN ROGERS SHOULDN'T HAVE WALKED AWAY FROM THE JOB.
BECAUSE THIS WORLD NEEDS A CAPTAIN AMERICA... MAYBE NOW MORE THAN EVER...
SO... HOW DO YOU WANT TO HANDLE THIS?
LEAVE HIM BE FOR NOW.
JUST TRACK HIM... FIND OUT WHERE HE GOT HIS POWER UPGRADE.

OF COURSE, THE NEW GUY IS RIGHT. THERE HAVE BEEN OTHERS WHO WORE MY UNIFORM...

WILLIAM NASLUND, THE SPIRIT OF '76, WAS THE FIRST...

...AND WHEN HE WAS KILLED, *JEFF MACE*, THE PATRIOT, COMPLETED HIS MISSION.

BUT NOT MANY CAN CARRY THE BURDEN...

DAILY-BUGLE

HAS CAP GONE CRAZY

March 23rd, 1954

OBIT

ROSCOE SIMONS

...NO MATTER HOW HARD THEY TRAIN OR HOW MUCH THEY WANT IT.

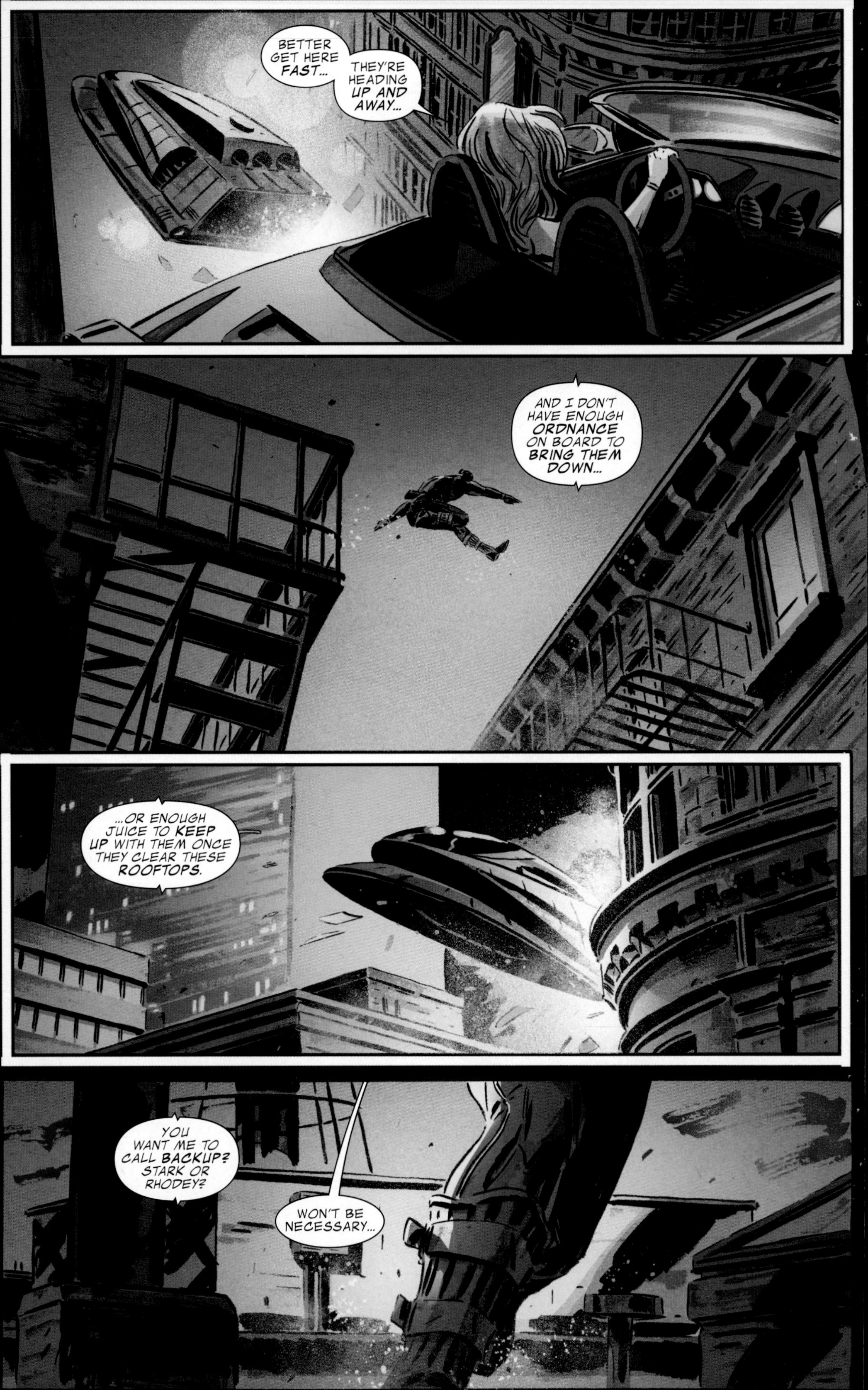
BETTER GET HERE FAST...
THEY'RE HEADING UP AND AWAY...
AND I DON'T HAVE ENOUGH ORDNANCE ON BOARD TO BRING THEM DOWN...
...OR ENOUGH JUICE TO KEEP UP WITH THEM ONCE THEY CLEAR THESE ROOFTOPS.
YOU WANT ME TO CALL BACKUP? STARK OR RHODEY?
WON'T BE NECESSARY...

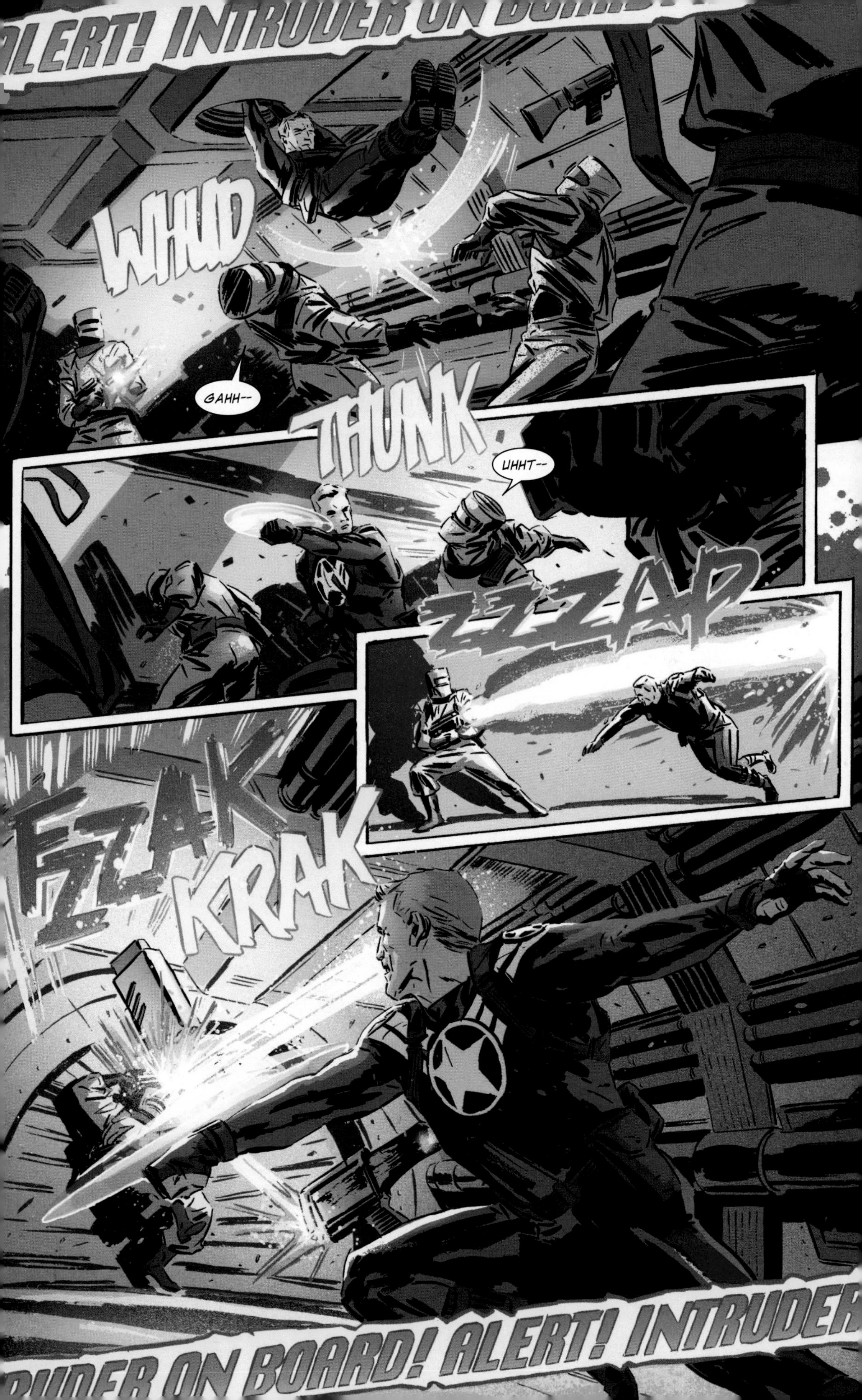
LERT! INTRUDER ON
WHUD
GAHH--
THUNK
UHHT--
ZZZZAP
FZZAK
KRAK
RUDER ON BOARD! ALERT! INTRUDER

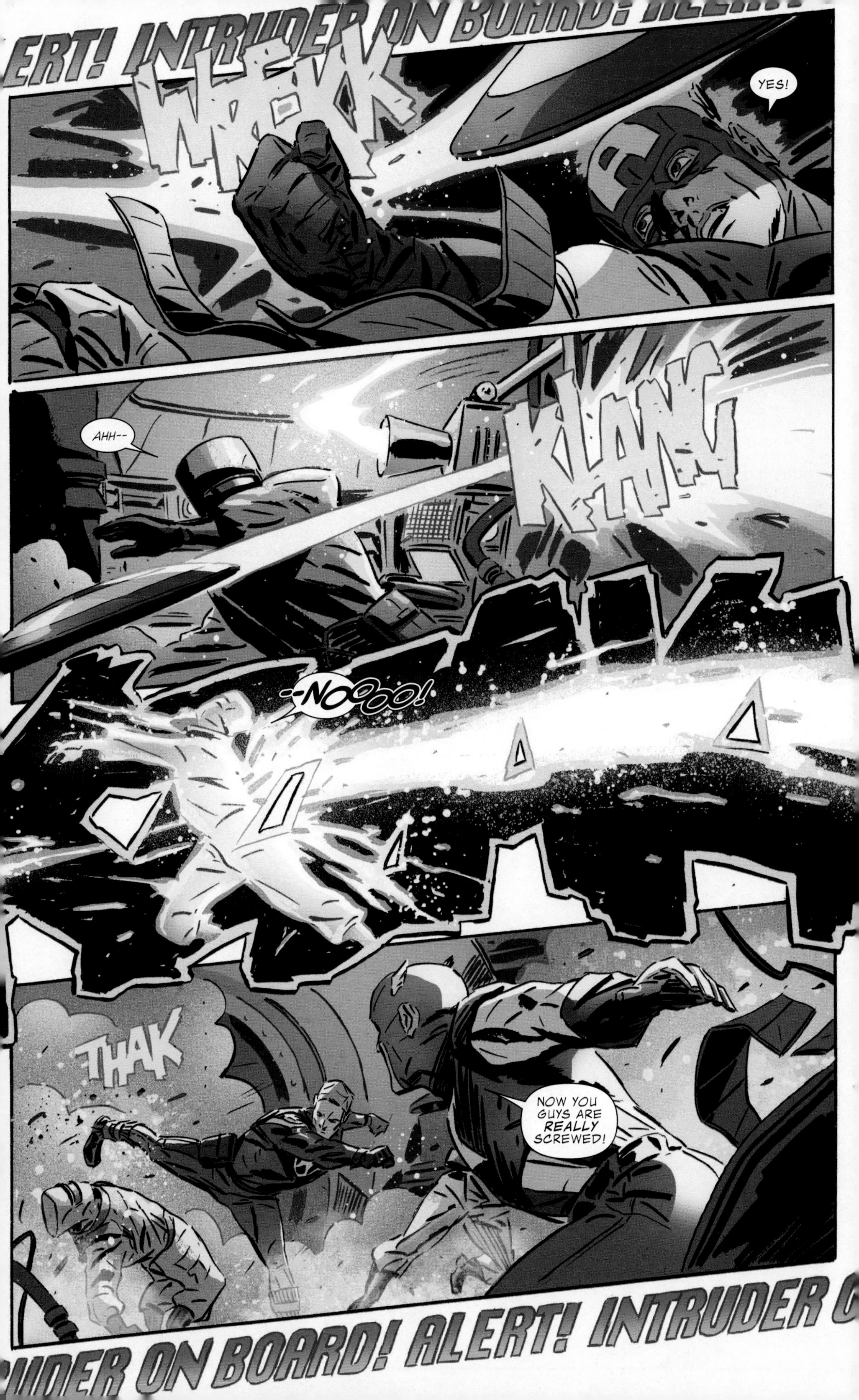
ERT! INTRUDER ON BOARD! ALERT!
WHEKK
YES!
AHH--
KLANG
--NOOOOO!
THAK
NOW YOU GUYS ARE REALLY SCREWED!
UDER ON BOARD! ALERT! INTRUDER O

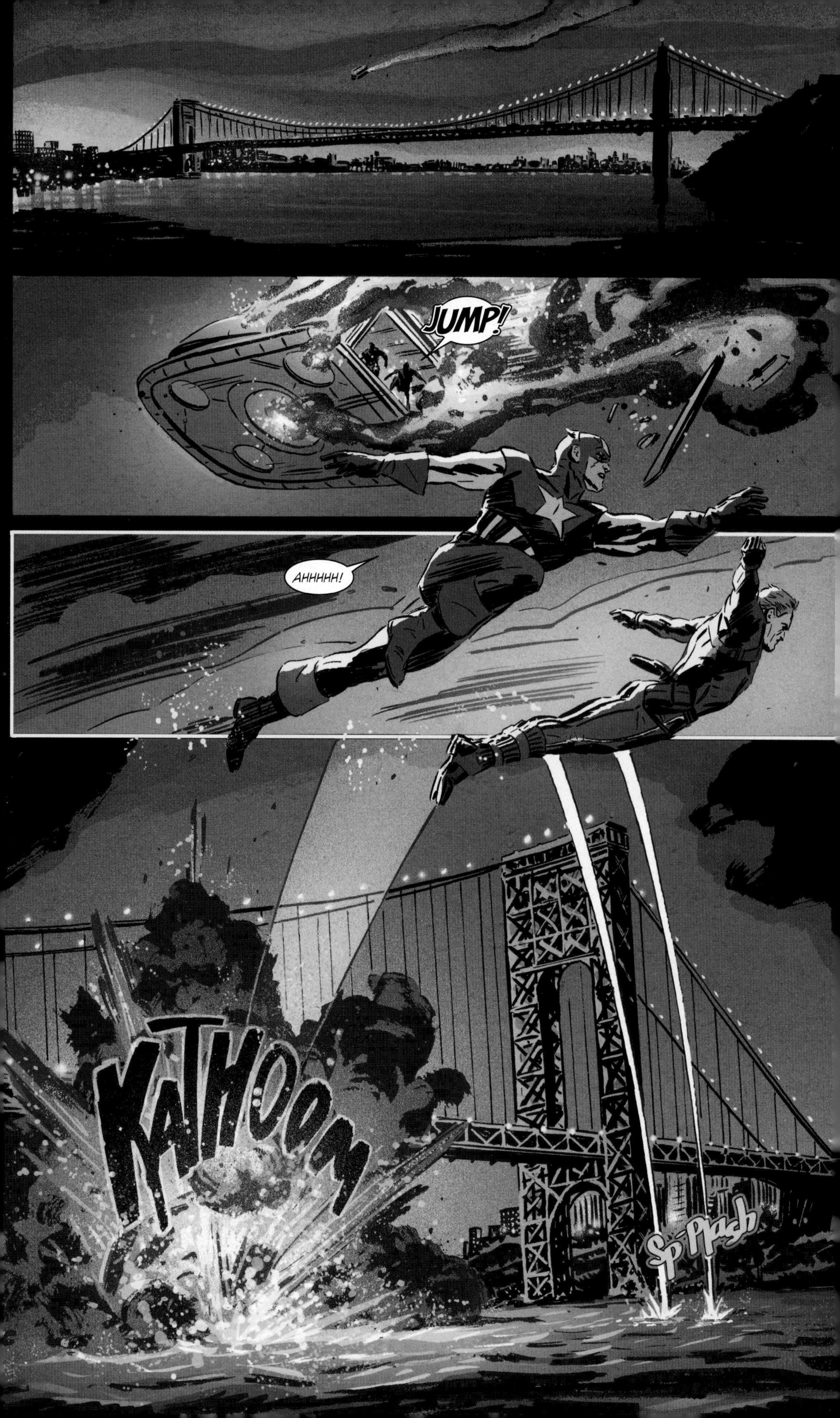

JUMP!
AHHHHH!
KATHOOM
Sp-Plash

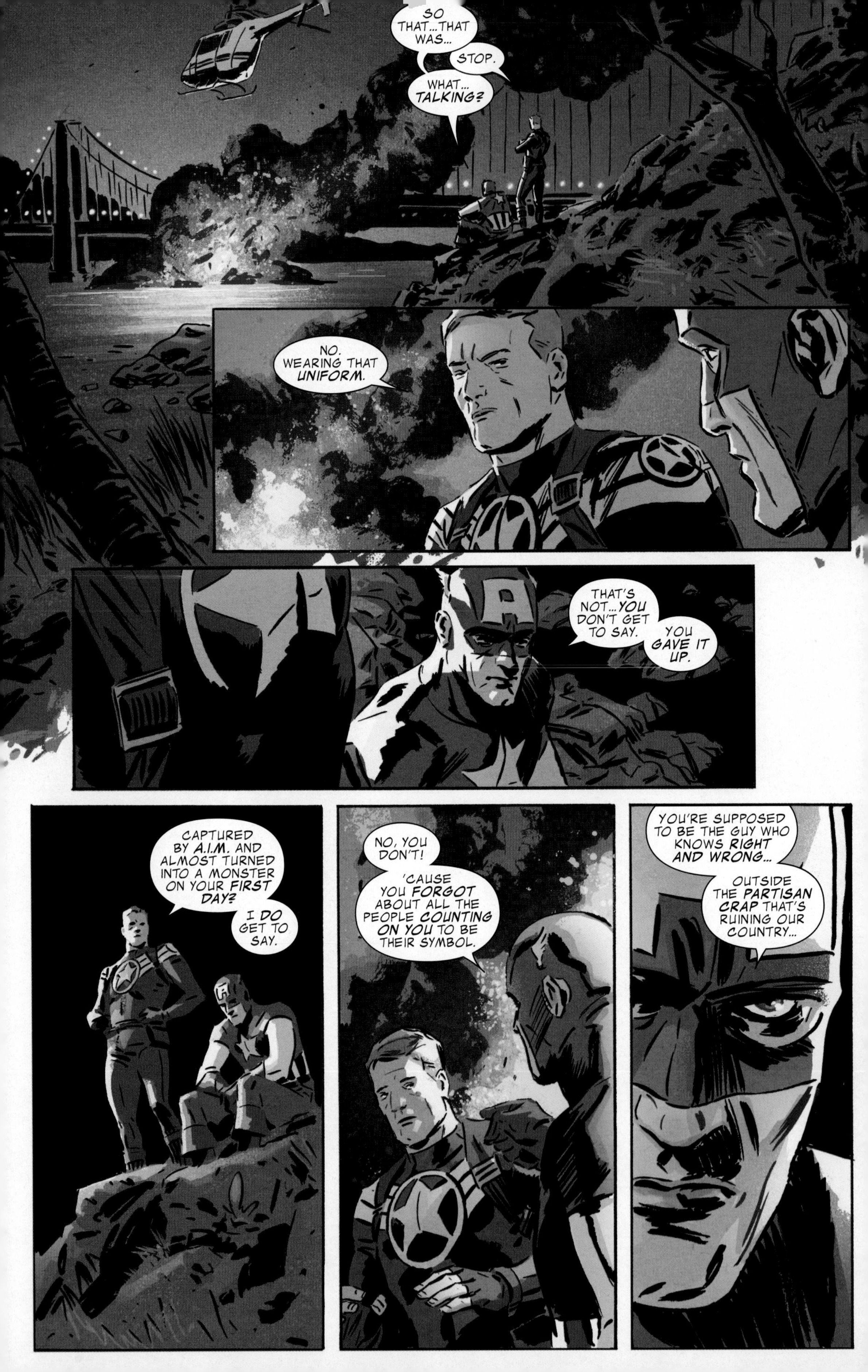
SO THAT...THAT WAS...
STOP.
WHAT... TALKING?
NO. WEARING THAT UNIFORM.
THAT'S NOT...YOU DON'T GET TO SAY.
YOU GAVE IT UP.
CAPTURED BY A.I.M. AND ALMOST TURNED INTO A MONSTER ON YOUR FIRST DAY?
I DO GET TO SAY.
NO, YOU DON'T!
'CAUSE YOU FORGOT ABOUT ALL THE PEOPLE COUNTING ON YOU TO BE THEIR SYMBOL.
YOU'RE SUPPOSED TO BE THE GUY WHO KNOWS RIGHT AND WRONG...
OUTSIDE THE PARTISAN CRAP THAT'S RUINING OUR COUNTRY...

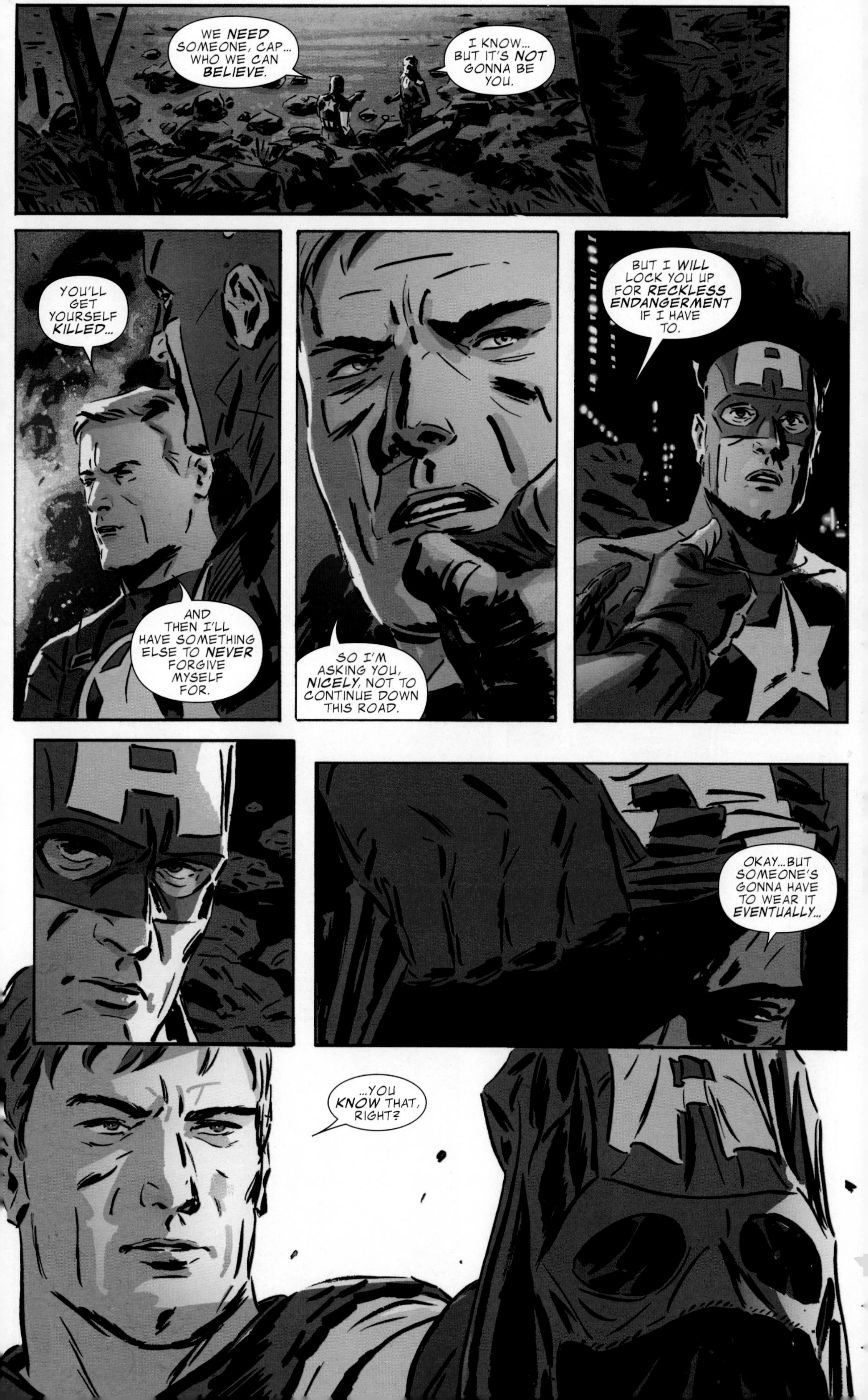
WE NEED SOMEONE, CAP... WHO WE CAN BELIEVE.
I KNOW... BUT IT'S NOT GONNA BE YOU.
YOU'LL GET YOURSELF KILLED...
AND THEN I'LL HAVE SOMETHING ELSE TO NEVER FORGIVE MYSELF FOR.
SO I'M ASKING YOU, NICELY, NOT TO CONTINUE DOWN THIS ROAD.
BUT I WILL LOCK YOU UP FOR RECKLESS ENDANGERMENT IF I HAVE TO.
OKAY...BUT SOMEONE'S GONNA HAVE TO WEAR IT EVENTUALLY...
...YOU KNOW THAT, RIGHT?

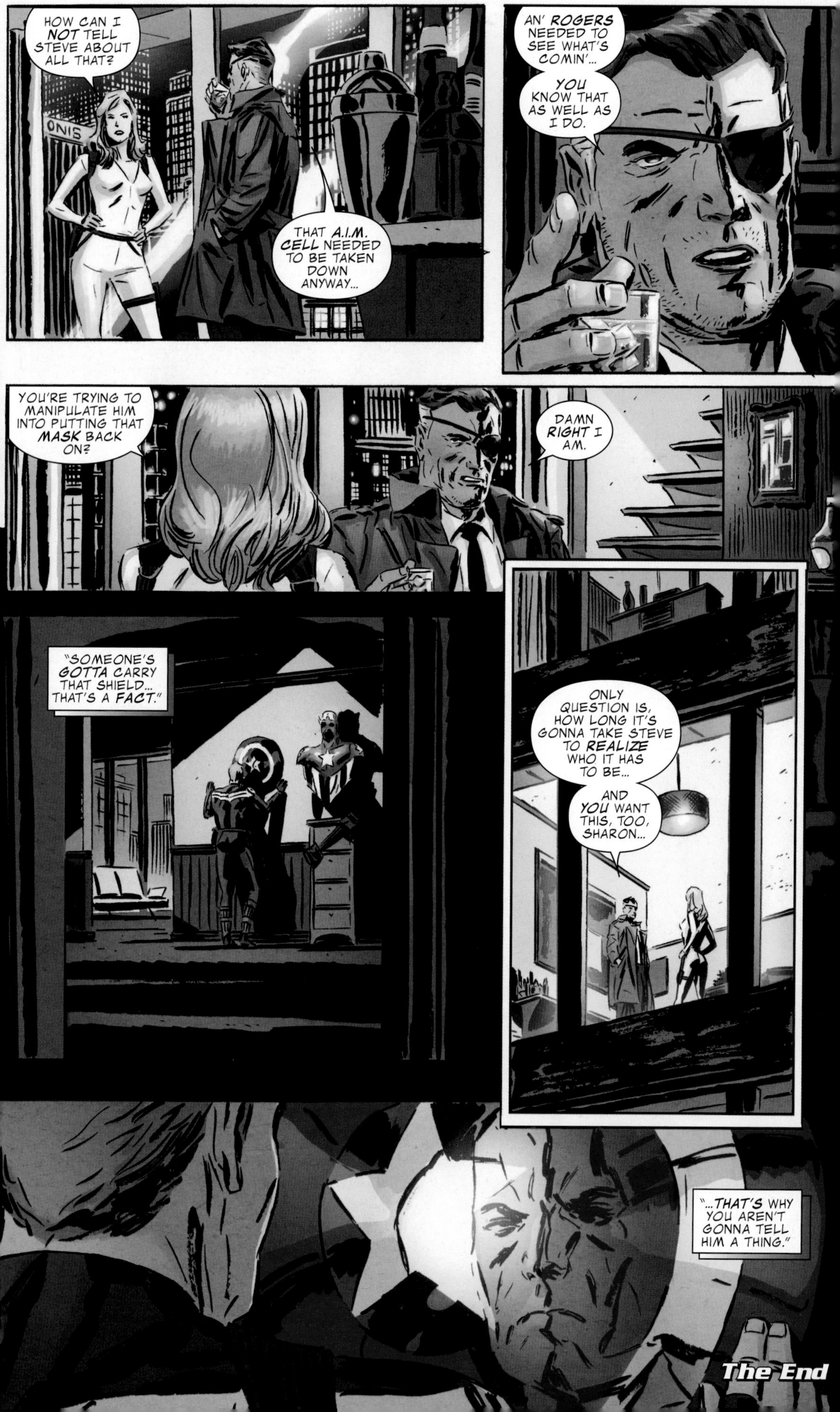

HOW CAN I NOT TELL STEVE ABOUT ALL THAT?
ONIS
THAT A.I.M. CELL NEEDED TO BE TAKEN DOWN ANYWAY...
AN' ROGERS NEEDED TO SEE WHAT'S COMIN'...
YOU KNOW THAT AS WELL AS I DO.
YOU'RE TRYING TO MANIPULATE HIM INTO PUTTING THAT MASK BACK ON?
DAMN RIGHT I AM.
"SOMEONE'S GOTTA CARRY THAT SHIELD... THAT'S A FACT."
ONLY QUESTION IS, HOW LONG IT'S GONNA TAKE STEVE TO REALIZE WHO IT HAS TO BE...
AND YOU WANT THIS, TOO, SHARON...
"...THAT'S WHY YOU AREN'T GONNA TELL HIM A THING."
The End